Also by the No Labels Foundation

No Labels:
A Shared Vision for a Stronger America

Just the Facts:
The First Step in Building a
National Strategic Agenda for America

Diversion Books
A Division of Diversion Publishing Corp.
443 Park Avenue South, Suite 1008
New York, New York 10016
www.DiversionBooks.com

For more information, email info@diversionbooks.com

First Diversion Books edition October 2015
Print ISBN: 978-1-68230-149-4
eBook ISBN: 978-1-62681-897-2

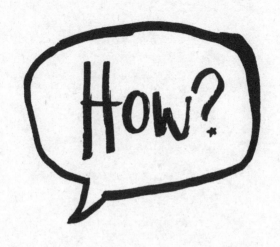

NO LABELS ANSWERS

THE MOST IMPORTANT QUESTION

OF THE 2016 ELECTION

Edited by
Governor Jon Huntsman
& Senator Joe Lieberman

Foreword By
Mack McLarty And Al Cardenas

DIVERSIONBOOKS

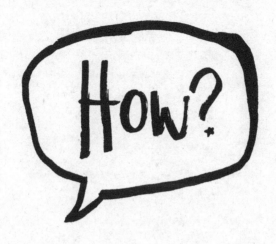

NO LABELS ANSWERS

THE MOST IMPORTANT QUESTION

OF THE 2016 ELECTION

Edited by
Governor Jon Huntsman
& Senator Joe Lieberman

Foreword By
Mack McLarty And Al Cardenas

DIVERSIONBOOKS

CONTENTS

FOREWORD:
COMMON SENSE PUT INTO ACTION

BY MACK MCLARTY AND AL CARDENAS
NO LABELS VICE CHAIRS

By the logic of today's Washington, we might look like a political Odd Couple: a centrist Democrat and a conservative Republican. One of us is a veteran of the Reagan and George H.W. Bush administrations and the other served in the Clinton administration. We are each loyal to our respective political party, and we have different philosophical foundations for addressing the nation's challenges. Certainly, we disagree on a number of issues.

But we're friends and partners in a burgeoning movement that is defined, not by what divides us, but by the common ground we believe is necessary to moving America forward. We share a deep commitment to collaboration, to finding solutions that both sides of the political divide are invested in and can believe in – solutions that this nation deserves and desperately needs.

That's the essence of No Labels. This organization provides a clear blueprint for cooperation and lays the foundation for governing, one outlined in the pages ahead. It doesn't advocate one set of policy initiatives over another. It doesn't ask elected officials to abandon party loyalties or principles. Instead, it presses our leaders to come to the table and engage with hard issues – and each other – and restore an attitude of pragmatic cooperation that has led to this nation's greatness. Best, of all, it provides specific guidelines for exactly *how* – *how* to solve problems together.

For generations, Americans looked to Washington to get things done. And Washington responded, especially in times of adversity – launching the New Deal during the Great Depression, harnessing the country's might in World War II, building the interstate highway system, winning the race for the moon, passing civil rights legislation, containing and defeating communism, supporting a long period of peacetime prosperity and rallying the nation after the attacks of September 11, 2001.

Each of these milestones, under Republican and Democratic administrations, had one thing in common: People with different political beliefs and ideas worked together.

Today, it's a different story. The adversarial, at times venomous, culture once limited to the campaign season now pervades the entire process of governance. What we used to call "gridlock" in Washington has calcified into dysfunction, a result of many factors including the way we finance campaigns, gerrymandering that creates "safe" districts for politicians, and the echo chamber of cable TV. Compromise and cooperation, bipartisanship and problem solving are almost nonexistent. Even civility is in short supply.

The result? Little gets done. The last five years have seen the two least productive Congresses in U.S. history. This dysfunction has had a devastating ripple effect on our fellow citizens and on the country. It has cost the economy an estimated one percent of GDP, and two million jobs since 2010. We have a spiraling budget deficit, stagnant wages, a broken immigration system. Small business, the engine of job creation, is sputtering, with more new businesses dying off than being created. Roads aren't being repaired. We have a tax code that's unintelligible to anyone without a CPA. With our leaders continually at loggerheads over crucial budget issues, we're subject to random, across-the-board cuts that hamper everything from lifesaving medical research to vital defense and national security projects.

This dysfunction deepens social and ideological divisions domestically and weakens us globally. It allows old problems to fester and opportunities for innovation to languish.

It's no wonder a staggering 80 percent of Americans believe the country is on the wrong track. Polls show that the main source of Americans' pessimism is not failures of policy, but failures of governance. They are hungry for leaders who can overcome paralyzing differences and work together to get things done.

How do we know there's a better way? Because we've seen it. We saw it in the 1980s when President Reagan and House Speaker Tip O'Neill worked across party lines to reform the tax code and protect Social Security. We saw it in the 1990s when President Clinton and House Speaker Newt Gingrich put aside differences to balance the budget. In both of those instances, and in other cases of great bipartisan achievement that you'll read about in the pages ahead, the two political opponents agreed on a goal first and then committed to a process to achieve it. Only after having the same finish line in sight did they begin working on the policy steps necessary to get them there.

These efforts were not always easy. They could be contentious, controversial, and as full of politicking and heated persuasion as any negotiations. But the difference was these leaders hung in there. They stayed at the table! They were invested in a big goal and committed to a process to achieve it.

We see that sort of goal-centered process at the state level, where many of our nation's governors, whether Republican or Democrat, forge productive relationships with evenly divided legislatures, work toward a common goal, and deliver for the citizens of their states.

But it's completely absent in Washington.

That needs to change. And No Labels is providing a roadmap. We are building support for a new framework for problem solving in which our leaders identify problems that need addressing and then, before doing anything else, agree to a set of goals to fix these problems.

That concept – setting a mutually agreed upon goal as a first step and then working on the policy specifics – is at the heart of No Label's big idea for a National Strategic Agenda, described in detail in the chapters that follow. It's a plan for *how* we move ahead as a nation.

Given the current climate in the nation's capital, we know it's easy to be cynical. It's tempting to dismiss as pie-in-the-sky any idea that involves across-the-aisle problem solving. But we're heartened by the remarkable strides No Label has already made toward this end. Last year, the No Labels Problem Solvers, a group of House and Senate members who meet regularly to build bridges across party lines and lead by example, became an official congressional organization called the Problem Solvers Caucus. This year, the organization's centerpiece proposal for a National Strategic Agenda was the subject of a Senate hearing and was introduced in both the House and Senate through bipartisan-backed resolutions. Active No Labels operations promoting this new framework for action are up and running in key presidential primary states.

All of these elements give us leverage to put our agenda squarely before the presidential candidates in the coming year and seek from them a full-throated commitment to bipartisan collaboration and problem solving. Without that, the next administration, whoever is in the driver's seat, will find it difficult to succeed.

We believe creating effective government is the most important task facing the country's next leader. No Labels offers a bold, but realistic pathway there. It begins with tearing down the barriers that prevent us from working together and changing course. It ends with solving our nation's problems through pragmatic cooperation.

We've seen in our long careers that common ground is often common sense put into action. That's the simple premise of No Labels. We're proud to be part of this most worthy pursuit.

PREFACE:
NO LABELS' MOMENT ARRIVES:
MAKING THE CASE FOR A
NATIONAL STRATEGIC AGENDA

On Wednesday, June 17, 2015, No Labels co-chairs Jon Huntsman and Joe Lieberman sat before the Senate Homeland Security and Governmental Affairs Committee and made the case for a National Strategic Agenda, a new problem-solving framework based on goals that both parties share. "This is a really important hearing," Sen. Ron Johnson, the Republican committee chairman from Wisconsin, told our team. "I think your efforts are extremely important. I love the fact you're starting with goals."

His Democratic counterpart, Sen. Tom Carper of Delaware, agreed: "You've given us a great agenda for our country."

This momentous day, with our leadership and our proposed agenda front and center before members of the U.S. Congress, was the culmination of years of work for No Labels and a validation of the worthiness and urgency of our mission.

Since our founding in 2010, we have worked to build a strong organization including a grassroots network of citizens and a coalition in Congress, both deeply committed to getting the partisan fighting and dysfunction out of our government. With input from the American people, Democrats, Republicans and independents, we came up with a bold, clear plan of action for a new framework for problem solving, a National Strategic Agenda, to address four key problems threatening the future prosperity and security of our nation.

This past spring, we made giant strides toward that goal, as Rep. Tom Reed, a New York Republican, and Rep. Ami Bera, a California Democrat, introduced a bipartisan resolution in the House proposing a National Strategic Agenda and calling on lawmakers of both parties and both chambers to make goal setting the first step in the governing process. The resolution stipulates that, before lawmakers get down to policy specifics, they would commit to pursuing four goals – unifying goals related to jobs, the budget, entitlements and energy security – and will do so in a spirit of cooperation that puts the urgent needs of the nation before party interests. (*www.congress.gov/114/ bills/hres207/BILLS-114hres207ih.pdf*)

Senators Bill Nelson, a Democrat from Florida, and John Thune, a South Dakota Republican, followed weeks later, introducing a companion resolution in the Senate. (*www.congress. gov/114/bills/sres199/BILLS-114sres199is.pdf*)

So far, more than 70 lawmakers have signed on as co-sponsors to these bills with support continuing to grow. These resolutions, if passed, would represent the first time Congress had adopted a specific methodology for solving the nation's problems.

The momentum for this proposal continued this year as the Homeland Security and Governmental Affairs committee invited No Labels to testify on the topic of "Governing Through Goal Setting," a major milestone for this organization and recognition that our common-sense mission is resonating, not only with citizens, but also with leaders in Washington. (You can read a full transcript of the hearing, including all testimony, at: *www.hsgac.senate.gov/hearings/governing-through-goal-setting-enhancing- the-economic-and-national-security-of-america*)

On that sunny day in June, our supporters – who had traveled to Capitol Hill from 22 states – packed the Dirksen hearing room as well as an overflow room. They watched our co-chairs, along with No Labels co-founder Andrew Tisch, co-chairman of Loews Corporation, and No Labels member Andrea Hogan, president and CEO of Merchants Metals, explain the premise of the National Strategic Agenda to the senators.

Sen. Lieberman, a former chairman of the committee he was appearing before, said the Agenda is an attempt to jumpstart the sort of across-the-aisle problem solving that happened naturally during much of his 24 years in Congress and provided the underpinning for the accomplishments of which he was most proud, ranging from the environment to national security to human rights legislation.

"To solve a problem – any problem – you need to set goals, get people to buy into those goals and put a process in place to achieve them," he told his former colleagues. "I personally believe a National Strategic Agenda is the best way to lift members out of the partisan morass and restore the bipartisan problem-solving spirit that is so badly needed here in Washington."

Co-chair Jon Huntsman painted a vivid portrait for the committee of how the process could work. He noted the growing congressional support for the resolutions, as well as the citizen armies that have been mobilized by No Labels in New Hampshire to ensure the National Strategic Agenda becomes a priority issue in the 2016 presidential race.

"Here's what the endgame looks like," Gov. Huntsman told the Senate panel. "A new president comes into office, having called in [his or her] campaign for the creation of a new National Strategic Agenda for the country. In the inaugural address, this new president promises to fly the congressional leaders from both parties down to Camp David … to start work on the Agenda.

"At Camp David, the president and the congressional leaders pick one of the goals to focus on and they commit to a process. They assign working groups or congressional committees to study the issues and suggest solutions. They agree to timelines and metrics for success. They agree to be accountable to one another and, above all, to the country. And they get to work, knowing that at least 50 members of the House and Senate have already gone on the record with a resolution saying they want to help create a National Strategic Agenda for America.

"Is this idea ambitious? Yes.

"Is it a total departure from how Washington has worked

for well over a decade? You bet.

"Is it impossible? Absolutely not."

The response to this bold idea has been, as Gov. Huntsman said, remarkable. On that day, senators praised our efforts, embracing our proposal for a National Strategic Agenda and sharing our belief that something different has to start happening in Washington. "I'm so encouraged by what you're trying to do," Chairman Johnson said.

Sen. Kelly Ayotte of New Hampshire said she was particularly impressed that the private sector, including business leaders such as Mr. Tisch and Ms. Hogan, were actively engaged in the process. Sen. Joni Ernst of Iowa applauded the particular set of issues the National Strategic Agenda attempts to tackle such as entitlement reform. "I'm thoroughly impressed with No Labels and its efforts for a National Strategic Agenda," the Iowa Republican said.

Days later, our movement was featured in a column in *The Washington Post* by editorial page editor Fred Hiatt, who hailed the National Strategic Agenda as "a new attempt to overcome the dysfunction (in Washington), so that the next president might not only get elected as a 'uniter' but govern as one, too."[1]

Our successful day before Congress, legislative action, and recognition by the national media bolstered our resolve and was the perfect springboard for our next step – our first ever National Problem Solver Convention on October 12, 2015 in New Hampshire, the largest gathering of undeclared voters of the campaign season.

The presidential candidates who attend and appear before this crowd of 1,000 New Hampshire voters will be asked about their commitment to the concept of bipartisan goal setting and problem solving.

These candidates – and *all* of the presidential candidates, in both parties – will be eligible to earn the No Labels Problem Solver Seal of Approval before the New Hampshire primary by

---

1 www.washingtonpost.com/opinions/no-labels-stakes-out-a-national-agenda/2015/06/28/e56f411c-1aa6-11e5-ab92-c75ae6ab94b5_story.html

committing to this framework for problem solving.

Their commitment means, very specifically, agreeing to meet with the leaders of both parties to settle on goals for the nation during the new president's first 30 days in office. (See chapter on "The No Labels Seal of Approval: Electing a Problem-Solver President" for more details.)

We think this Seal of Approval could prove to be the winning ticket in New Hampshire. In the Granite State, more than 40 percent of the vote comes from undeclared voters, who are eligible to vote in that state's primary and who are especially enthusiastic about the No Labels message and our call for a National Strategic Agenda.

We are confident that more and more voters, in New Hampshire and all across the country, will be demanding this kind of commitment from the candidates they meet and hear from. These candidates are always happy to tell us what they *want* to do. But in the 2016 election, *want* simply won't cut it. We believe it is time to demand a real strategy for *how* they will unite a divided nation behind big goals to solve our common problems. And we believe the answer to this "how" question can be found with a groundbreaking idea that comes straight from the American people, and that is outlined in this book.

The citizens of this country recognize that only with a goal-oriented, consensus-seeking, problem-solving leader in the Oval Office will January 2017 mark the beginning of a new day in Washington and a new era of growth and prosperity for the nation. We stand ready to help make that happen.

— *Nancy Jacobson, Clarine Nardi Riddle,*
Dr. Bill Galston, Rep. Tom Davis,
No Labels Co-Founders

SHARED VISION, COMMON GOALS: A BETTER FRAMEWORK FOR PROBLEM SOLVING

BY GOVERNOR JON HUNTSMAN

AND SENATOR JOE LIEBERMAN

NO LABELS HONORARY CO-CHAIRS

Which country represents the greatest danger to the United States?

That was the question the Pew Research Center asked more than a thousand Americans in November 2013. Participants weren't given a list of options; they were just asked to name their choice. The top of the list wasn't particularly surprising; in a world of nuclear threats and economic warfare, Iran and China were obvious choices. But the next country named was more of a shock. According to the American people, the third country on the list of America's greatest enemies was America itself.[2]

How did we get here? How did we get to a place where the American people have concluded that we are literally one of our own worst enemies?

Maybe it was when our leaders in Washington turned running our government into an exercise in chaos and uncertainty, flailing from one late-night crisis to another, closing last minute deals, or shutting down the government when they failed to reach an agreement. Maybe it was when the president's sweeping health care law passed without a single Republican

---

2 www.people-press.org/files/legacy-questionnaires/12-3-13%20 APW%20VI%20Topline%20for%20Release.pdf

vote. Or maybe it was when Republicans responded by resorting to unprecedented, even dangerous, tactics to try to roll it back.

When the American people look to Washington, they see a city divided. Two parties who don't meet together, eat together, or even seem to like each other. Two sides that never even *try* to work together. Different teams who never lay out a common agenda to strengthen our country. Instead, there are two separate visions and two separate agendas – with a constant war of attack ads, vitriol, and all-around drama standing between them.

The more Americans hear about what's happening in Washington, the more convinced they become that our best days are behind us. And it's hard to blame them. But luckily, even though Washington is filled with America's representatives, its dysfunction does not represent America. And if you look at America as a whole, there are a lot more reasons to feel optimistic.

Yes, we have big challenges to face as a country. In the last 18 years, we went from a balanced budget to record, unsustainable deficits. We still promise our children that Social Security and Medicare will be there for them, but we don't take the steps to guarantee that. Meanwhile, we're still climbing back from a recession that cost us millions of jobs, shrank our economy, and shattered our sense of economic security. We know that harnessing a new energy economy could create countless jobs and unleash amazing economic growth – but we still don't have a clear energy policy to take advantage of the opportunity.

The challenges are real. No one disputes that. But these challenges are also solvable. Not in theory, or in the abstract. The solutions are out there – and it's not too late for our leaders to come together and pass them into law.

It might surprise you to hear that despite all the noise and rancor coming out of Washington, there are still plenty of people on both sides of the aisle who *want* to solve problems. From the staunchest conservatives to the most committed liberals, our elected leaders care deeply about this country. And for the most part, they're more discouraged than anyone that our two parties just can't seem to get to "yes" anymore.

So what's the problem? Bold systemic reform ideas like

getting money out of politics or putting an end to congressional gerrymandering are certainly worthy and important endeavors – but they are tough, multiyear, state-by state slogs. Ideas like that may never come to fruition – or come in time. Because the simple fact is that we need a better governing system that takes advantages of the best impulses in Washington, not the worst. And we need it *today*.

The good news is that we can start changing the system right away. Common ground in Washington really *does* exist if only our leaders are empowered to find it. Our leaders really can be problem solvers again – they just need a governing process that brings them together instead of pulling them apart.

At No Labels, we've seen a vision of how our government can work. We're a citizens movement of Democrats, Republicans, and Independents dedicated to a new politics of problem solving. Our membership includes members of Congress from both sides of the aisle, academics, business leaders, and hundreds of thousands of citizens from every corner of our country. They don't agree on everything, but they definitely agree that we need our leaders to stop fighting and start working together again.

This is exactly what the American people are calling for. We surveyed them in a poll in 2015, and *97 percent* of Americans said it was important that our next president be a problem solver. These days, it's impossible to get 97 percent of Americans to agree on the toppings for a free pizza, or much of anything else – but in this case, they were nearly unanimous. We *need* our leaders to be problem solvers once again – and all of us know it.

In this book, we build on No Labels' work to create a national constituency for problem solving by offering a path forward for changing American politics. In the pages ahead, you'll hear from leaders from every part of American life – from business, government, economics, and academia. You'll hear from Problem Solver members of Congress who want to work across the aisle and get things done.

These contributors come from different places and backgrounds, but they lent their perspectives and their voices to this book because they all believe that we need to do better as a country. We need to actually know where we're going – and we need to work together to get there.

Our campaign to change American politics aims to put an end to a governing process that simply drifts between divisive debates, political posturing, and outright crises. Instead, we want to replace all that with a problem- solving process. And that starts with forging a National Strategic Agenda for our country.

Think about the State of the Union. It's a moment when a president is supposed to gauge where we stand as a country – and where we need to go. But these days, no matter which party holds the Oval Office, these addresses are mainly just laundry lists detailing the agenda of one party. The president announces priorities, and then the other side jumps up in protest. Before long, we're mired in gridlock – and neither side ever achieves much of anything at all.

If we had a National Strategic Agenda, this could all be different. The president and the leader of the opposition would meet before the State of the Union to agree on goals to pursue over the next year. It would shift the focus to setting shared goals – and the entire process would be recast. Now, the two sides would reach agreement on goals *before* the policymaking process starts. And instead of constantly getting jammed up in gridlock, both sides would have a shared end to work toward once the negotiations start.

No Labels is charting this new way forward. Like every initiative No Labels has proposed, this National Strategic Agenda is a product of discussion and agreement from every part of the political spectrum. It will require leaders to come together to explore the shared goals that most Americans, whatever their politics, whatever their labels, believe are vital to the well-being and growth of our country.

If we can forge agreement on a national agenda – based on mutually agreed upon objectives – we can finally start to break the gridlock in our politics today. That's a path forward that both parties should rally around. Because we can't keep muddling along like we are now. It's time to start solving problems again. It's time to get down to work. It's time to stop fighting and start fixing.

STOP FIGHTING, START FIXING:
THE NO LABELS STORY

I believe that we can change politics in America for a simple reason: I've already seen No Labels' incredible progress toward bringing our leaders together. No Labels launched the only organized forum in Washington for members of different parties in Congress to come together, talk openly about the challenges we face, and discuss the range of possible solutions. The ideological spectrum represented in these meetings is as vast as our country itself – but when folks sit down at that table, they're ready to solve problems together. In this chapter, the No Labels co-founders tell the story of how it all began – and what's coming next.

– Jon Huntsman

The No Labels co-founders were as anxious and jittery as candidates on an election night as they made their way to Alfred J. Lerner Hall on the cold New York morning of December 13, 2010.

Driven by a firm belief that our political system was badly broken – and an instinct that much of America shared their frustration – the veteran political advisers and elected officials had spent the previous year laying the groundwork for a new organization that would push back against the culture of extreme partisanship and acrimony that was gripping Washington. These Democrats and Republicans, some of the most experienced and respected political minds in America, had traveled the country – to libraries, college campuses, living rooms and coffee shops – to plant the seeds for a new movement among citizens of all political stripes.

Now the day of the official launch had finally arrived. The

founding leaders had set an audacious goal: to get 1,000 people from all 50 states to come to New York – on their own dime! – for the kickoff of No Labels, a new grassroots organization that would put problem solving and the good of the country ahead of partisan politics.

They'd lined up an impressive array of speakers and panels (even a Broadway star to sing the national anthem), purchased box lunches for the expected crowd, and invited reporters to cover the day-long event.

But as the No Labels founders made their way to Columbia University on that raw December morning, they held their breath.

They had built the organization. Would the people actually come?

HOW TO BUILD A NETWORK FOR PROBLEM SOLVING

It had been easy for No Labels co-founder Nancy Jacobson, for nearly three decades an adviser and fundraiser for major Democratic Senate and presidential candidates, to find fellow political professionals who were as disenchanted with the breakdown in Washington as she was and eager to find a way to build bridges across the partisan divide.

For years, the gulf between the two parties had been growing, with partisan poison preventing action on the urgent issues of the day, from the budget to the entitlement reform, often bringing the government to a complete halt. The election of President Obama had offered real promise for a new day of cooperation and unity. But by 2010 that hope had vanished when the Affordable Care Act passed in the House, just as it had in the Senate three months earlier, without a single Republican vote, and the flames of vitriol and hyperpartisanship raged hotter than ever. Special interest groups fanned those partisan fires, promoting divisions and rewarding bad behavior.

Outside Washington, the Tea Party was staking out terrain on the conservative side, Moveon.org on the progressive side. In the vast space occupied by those who wanted their elected officials to work together and get things done – most Americans

– there was nothing.

Jacobson found a kindred spirit on the other side of the aisle in Mark McKinnon, a leading Republican strategist who had worked for President George W. Bush and Senator John McCain, and had for years seen the optimistic, reformist hopes of well-meaning politicians crumble in the harsh partisan light of Washington. He too believed there was a hearty appetite throughout the country for better behavior among elected officials – for real collaboration and problem solving.

Jacobson and McKinnon reached out to their respective networks, and soon a long list of like-minded political veterans and presidential advisers were in: Bill Galston, a former deputy domestic policy adviser to President Clinton who had long embraced a politics of consensus building; journalist and author John Avlon, who'd been chief speechwriter for former New York mayor Rudy Giuliani; Clarine Nardi Riddle, a former Connecticut attorney general and chief of staff to Sen. Joe Lieberman; former House Republican Tom Davis of Virginia; former Kentucky State Treasurer Jonathan Miller; former Atlanta City Council President Lisa Borders; and David Walker, U.S. Comptroller General under Presidents Clinton and Bush.

The mission also attracted civic-minded business leaders such as Panera Bread founder Ron Shaich and Loews Corp. co-chairman Andrew Tisch. They joined the cause – and the No Labels movement was off and running.

Over several months, these and other thought leaders crafted the vision for No Labels, drawing up a blueprint for a new political infrastructure that would promote problem solving. The gridlock had become so perilous that the founders wanted an action- and results-oriented agenda. They wanted to have immediate impact, so they would leave the systemic changes requiring long-term solutions – such as campaign finance, redistricting, and electoral reforms – to other groups already grappling with such issues. Instead, they would seek rule and process changes – immediate fixes to the system that were palatable to both parties, would bring about real change, lower the ideological temperature, and could be achieved right away.

No Labels would respect the two-party system, embracing the most devoted Democrats and the most stalwart Republicans, the most ardent conservatives and the most passionate liberals. Everyone would have a place at the table, as long as they were committed to putting their country first and working in good faith with the other side.

Finally, the founders made one last decision that became a hallmark of the organization. Though No Labels would be based in Washington – in the early days, a one-bedroom apartment so crammed that one work station was in the bathroom shower – this would be a citizen-driven movement, its energy harnessed from Americans who wanted their elected leaders to do better. Without the voices of the people, politicians in Washington would never pay attention. So throughout 2010, the founders took No Labels on the road, fanning out throughout the country like a primary presidential campaign to drum up support and fine-tune the mission.

FROM KITCHEN TABLES TO NATIONAL MEETINGS: A GRASSROOTS MOVEMENT GROWS

No one had to tell the teacher in Des Moines or the social worker in Little Rock that the system was broken. Everyone knew it. And they were starved for the sort of common sense approach to tackling the nation's problems that No Labels was all about.

In Minneapolis, Laurence Reszetar, a young lawyer, had become increasingly depressed and apathetic about politics. He'd grown up in a military family that valued politics, and he eventually became an official in the state Democratic-Farmer-Labor Party. But in the last several years, he'd become disenchanted, especially after getting flak for supporting a St. Paul City Council candidate who wasn't the party favorite. He felt such extreme party allegiance was dominating the system, from the local level to the national level, where it often led to stalemates and inaction. No one swears an oath to their party, he thought, yet politicians act as if they do. Looking down at his two-year-old daughter and newborn son, Reszetar felt he owed it to his children's generation to hit the reset button.

Lifelong Republican Ted Buerger, an Internet entrepreneur in Westchester, NY, was similarly disillusioned by all the fighting and divisiveness that he felt was preventing any real progress. The passage of Obama's health care bill with Democrats alone seemed to him the symbol of everything that was wrong with politics. Members of Congress had told him there was so much rancor in Washington that it was increasingly dangerous for them to be photographed with colleagues from the opposite party. Buerger knew there had to be a better way to govern.

In Dallas, personal stylist Bobbi Schwartz, a self-described Goldwater/Reagan-style Republican, would often call or write her representative in Congress with strongly held views – often frustration – about the direction of the country and inaction in Washington. She never expected any results. As a small business owner, she felt that if people in the private sector performed as poorly as members of Congress, they'd be fired. When she happened upon a discussion of No Labels on C-SPAN in 2010, she was glued to the television – and hooked. She sent out an email to everyone she knew, telling them that finally, there was a way to do something beyond randomly calling your representative. Finally, there was a way to be heard and try to effect change.

People like Reszetar, Buerger, and Schwartz – and eventually about 100 other local leaders – built the network from the ground up, holding meetings around their kitchen tables or at their neighborhood libraries.

Toward the end of 2010, the grassroots buzz about No Labels was reaching elected officials, such as the newly elected junior senator from West Virginia, Joe Manchin, the state's former Democratic governor who'd long been committed to problem solving. Senator Manchin decided he not only wanted to be a part of this new movement, but to do whatever he could to get it off the ground.

He made his way to New York for the launch of No Labels, joining other senators, House members, a governor, big city mayors and other current and former political figures – as well as citizens from all across America.

When the founders looked out to the audience at Columbia's Lerner Hall, they saw a retired police officer from Alaska, a restaurant owner from Louisiana, a physical therapist from New Hampshire, students from Boston College and the University of Texas.

They saw that the citizens had indeed come – more than 1,000 of them, in fact, from all 50 states – some with their families, some from halfway around the continent, all with a determination to get the country moving forward again, and all with a belief that their voices could make a difference.

THE NEXT STEP: TURNING IDEAS INTO ACTION

Since that day, the No Labels network has grown to more than half a million citizens, with leaders and organizations in every state calling on their political leaders to work together to solve the nation's problems. Only two people showed up to the first meeting Laurence Reszetar held at the Washburn Library in Minneapolis. But the next time out, he had an audience of 50, and by September 2013, he filled the Westminster Presbyterian Church with 500 people for a No Labels town hall meeting that was broadcast on public radio.

When Senator Manchin looked for a Republican counterpart to lead the organization in those early days, he found a politician equally passionate about changing the dynamics of politics: Jon Huntsman, a fellow former governor from Utah. With the Democratic senator and the former Republican governor and presidential candidate at the helm, No Labels in three short years took the concepts of consensus building and problem solving and transformed them from verboten utterances in Washington to words that have gained such currency they will assuredly be on the lips of every candidate as we enter a new presidential campaign cycle. Eventually, Sen. Manchin handed the reins of No Labels to another reform-minded politician, former Sen. Joe Lieberman, who joined Gov. Huntsman in 2014 as honorary co-chair.

No Labels has proven that, with an infrastructure for cooperation – something as simple as establishing regular meetings for members of Congress of both parties to come together, talk to each other and build trust – problem solving works.

The group has produced a series of non-ideological initiatives – many of them simple, common-sense rule and process changes to get the system moving – that have garnered support from both parties and gained traction.

One of the first ideas, No Budget No Pay, was a proposal to withhold lawmakers' paychecks if they can't make spending and budget decisions on time. It became so popular that an entire Senate hearing was devoted to the idea. It became a winning campaign agenda item for California Rep. Ami Bera, who unseated a three-term congressman who had opposed the idea. Ultimately, a version of No Budget No Pay, part of No Labels' Make Congress Work! package (*www.nolabels.org/work*), was signed into law by President Obama in February 2013.

Two other reform packages followed: Make the Presidency Work! (*www.nolabels.org/presidency-work*), a prescription for enhancing the power and accountability of the Oval Office occupant, and Make Government Work! (*www.nolabels.org/make-government-work*), a package of nine initiatives to reduce government wate and inefficiency that evolved into 18 separate pieces of legislation in the House and Senate. One of those bills, 21st Century Healthcare for Heroes, which proposed merging the electronic records of the Department of Defense and Veterans Administration to better serve our military heroes, was incorporated into the 2013 Defense Appropriations legislation and signed into law.

These initiatives have proven that members of different parties can still come together around legislation based on common-sense problem solving.

As the No Labels leaders and supporters have worked to build support for their agenda, they've attracted more and more allies on Capitol Hill, lawmakers who've been frustrated by their inability to work with colleagues across the aisle. These consensus-minded senators and House members banded together to form the No Labels Problem Solvers, a coalition that met regularly and was committed to putting the best interests of the country ahead of partisan point scoring.

During the 2013 government shutdown, the Problem Solvers met daily, often in the cold, windowless basement of a Tex-Mex restaurant on Capitol Hill, to try to come up with ideas for breaking the deadlock. As Rep. Charlie Dent of Pennsylvania writes about in this volume, the No Labels Problem Solvers came up with a plan that became central to the Senate's successful negotiations.

These members also connected with state and local officials, helping to build a dynamic No Labels network across the country that is engaging everyone from big city mayors to college students to thought leaders.

By 2014, the Problem Solvers coalition had become such a formidable force it was formalized into an official congressional organization – the Problem Solvers Caucus, now nearly 60 members strong – the first one ever dedicated to bipartisan consensus building.

A NATIONAL STRATEGIC AGENDA
FOR AMERICA'S NEXT PRESIDENT

With a burgeoning nationwide network, a significant congressional presence, and ideas that have earned notice and praise in newspapers all over the country including *The New York Times*, *The Washington Post* and *The Wall Street Journal*, No Labels took its next bold step in 2014 with a call for a National Strategic Agenda – and a new, better process for governing and problem solving. If you're reading this book, you're already a part of it.

The idea for a National Strategic Agenda came from the recognition of a number of stark political realities: 1) many of the forces that lead to hyperpartisanship, such as the way campaigns are financed, redistricting, and the polarizing nature of media, are not about to change anytime soon; 2) what is needed is a mechanism or process that will promote – in fact, *require* – across-the-aisle problem solving within today's partisan culture; 3) this process will only work with buy-in from both the president and a critical mass in Congress; 4) that buy-in is only likely to occur if citizens demand it from their elected officials, starting with the newly elected president; and 5) the great bipartisan achievements of the past occurred when both sides worked toward the same goal.

With those political truths in mind, No Labels conducted polling and sought input from business leaders, academics, and policy experts across the country on the most urgent issues of the day. All of that research pointed to four goals that make up the pillars of the National Strategic Agenda: creating 25 million net new jobs in the next decade, securing Medicare and Social Security for the next 75 years, balancing the federal budget by 2030 and achieving energy security by 2024.

Although the National Strategic Agenda is focused on these big policy goals, it is not a policy plan. We are not asking our next president and Congress to endorse specific policies. Instead, we are asking them to invest in a new process for problem solving.

No Labels is asking 2016 presidential candidates to embrace the National Strategic Agenda and to commit, if elected, to begin work with a bipartisan group of congressional leaders on at least one of the four goals within the first 30 days of their administration. Presidential candidates who publicly make this commitment will receive the No Labels Problem Solvers Seal of Approval.

When the next president enters office, it will be critically important to have members of Congress willing to get to work on a National Strategic Agenda. That's why No Labels is aggressively recruiting allies on Capitol Hill, with over 70 members as of August 2015 having endorsed congressional resolutions (H.Res. 207 and S.Res. 199) calling for a new National Strategic Agenda for America.

These resolutions, as well as a Senate hearing this past June, have given this idea the necessary legislative authority. Bolstered by a strong No Labels operation in the early presidential voting state of New Hampshire, the Agenda is well on its way to widespread support and a central role in the campaign debate.

If ever there was a moment for such a national agenda, and for a movement like No Labels, it is now. The original founders have grown only more convinced over the last several years that the continued discord and dysfunction in Washington threatens progress and prosperity. Out of nothing but sheer dedication to their country, they continue to commit their own time and resources to No Labels, bringing valuable lessons learned from years in the White House, congressional offices or campaigns to our political landscape today.

Their vision for what could be – and what should be – also attracts legions of young people from all over who want leaders they can be proud of. There are now No Labels chapters on 110 college campuses. And the organization has become a magnet for scores of college interns who come through its doors each year to be a part of this important movement that speaks so clearly to their generation.

But the heartbeat of No Labels is still a fast-growing citizen army that is telling its leaders every day that they need to do better. They need to put their partisan labels aside and put America first. And they need to start today.

HOW TO CHANGE
AMERICAN POLITICS:
WE CAN MOVE FORWARD
IF WE AGREE WHERE TO GO

Getting things done in Washington has never been easy. But not long ago, it was at least possible. At a time when our nation has so many unaddressed and pressing problems, it's imperative we get back to an efficient, accountable, responsive government. In this chapter, the No-Labels co-founders examine some of the problems with our governing dynamics today – and they explain what needs to change so we can create a problem-solving government once again.

– Joe Lieberman

The stadium was packed by 10 a.m. Despite the burning Texas sun and the stifling humidity, 40,000 people jammed into Houston's Rice Stadium on a fateful morning in September 1962. It's not clear how many in the crowd knew that they were there to witness one of the most important speeches of the 20th century – but by the time President John Fitzgerald Kennedy was finished speaking, there was little doubt that our nation had entered the first moment in a new era of American history.

"We choose to go to the moon," the president said. "We choose to go to the moon in this decade and do the other things, not because they are easy, but because they are hard, because that goal will serve to organize and measure the best of our energies and skills, because that challenge is one that we are willing to accept, one we are unwilling to postpone, and one which we intend to win."[3]

At the time, it wasn't fully clear how we planned to achieve this objective. But as President Kennedy said, simply setting the goal was the first critical step toward success. A goal that, as he said, "will serve to organize and measure the best of our energies and skills."

Of course, he was right. Within a decade, we had gathered our resources, brought together our best minds, and stood together as a nation as an American flag was planted on the surface of the moon.

We achieved this historic accomplishment because President Kennedy understood how important it was to bring the country together around a shared sense of purpose. He understood that goals dispel passivity and inspire action. They bring seemingly impossible feats just within our grasp. And that's the same reason that we need a new set of shared American goals today.

We know this might sound like a pie-in-the-sky dream. After all, there have been plenty of well-intentioned movements to change politics before – and a lot of them haven't gotten very far. But our campaign is different. We know it's not enough to just offer nice words about civility and bipartisanship. We know there are plenty of people on both sides with strongly-held beliefs – and we don't expect to change that.

Instead, our campaign is based around a simple concept: Right now, all of the dynamics in Washington create a constant battle between two sides. More and more, it seems our leaders are only focused on the short-term pressures of the moment: the next legislative battle, the next election, the next day's headlines.

That's what we need to change. We need to build a governing infrastructure that actually encourages our leaders to solve problems. And we can start that process today.

---

3 www.chron.com/news/nation-world/article/50-years-ago-Kennedy-reached-for-stars-in-3852085.php

THE "PROBLEM SOLVING" INFRASTRUCTURE

If you look at the governing process in Washington right now, you'll see that most of our elected leaders are determined to govern in a zero-sum, "winner-take-all" manner. But with America divided, both sides need to recognize that neither party can just dominate the other or get everything they want. That's not real leadership – and we'll never get anything done that way.

Instead, we need a governing process that starts with a basic recognition: In an era of divided government, we can only move forward if we can agree on where we need to go. That's why we need a mechanism that pushes the different parties to come together around a shared direction for our country.

Even when Washington has been bitterly divided in the past, common goals have helped turn confrontation into agreement. They change the dialogue, shifting the issue from *whether* we should do something to *how* we can do it. With that simple shift, both sides suddenly have a shared basis to evaluate competing proposals and collaborate to make tradeoffs between them.

As you'll see in the next chapter, leaders with views as divergent as Bill Clinton, Ronald Reagan, Tip O'Neill, and Newt Gingrich, have proven this point. Neither side got everything it wanted in any of these instances, but once party leaders agreed where they wanted to go, they found a way to get there together.

Or look at what happened in 1919, when a young army officer joined a convoy designed to test whether America's roads would permit the movement of troops and equipment from coast to coast. He wrote a vivid report of his experiences, and he never forgot how slow the trip was, or how many times trucks skidded off poorly maintained surfaces.

Thirty three years later, this officer, now a military hero, ran for president, denouncing the condition of America's roads and calling for the creation of an interstate highway system. Although he was known as a cautious and conservative man, Dwight Eisenhower said this: "I see an America where a mighty network of highways spreads across our country." After winning the presidency, Eisenhower used the full powers of his presidency to transform this vision into a national goal, telling Congress in 1955 that "Our unity as a nation is sustained by free communication of thought and by easy transportation of people and goods." After tough negotiations about transforming this goal into reality, he signed the Highway Act of 1956. Today, that "mighty network" forms the backbone of our nation, and generations of Americans can't even imagine our nation without it.

Today's challenges may be different, but our country's need for shared purposes remains. That's why No Labels is working to identify shared goals so we can formulate a National Strategic Agenda.

The American people know we can't afford to go on the way we've been going. They're demanding a new politics of problem solving – and now is the time to forge it. If we don't, the alternative is continued gridlock, stagnation, and decline. If we want to pass on a strong, prosperous, secure nation to our children, we must change course. And we have no time to waste.

NO LABELS VOICES
REP. LYNN JENKINS (R-KS)

When I first arrived in Washington in 2009, the Democrats controlled the House and the Senate and President Obama had just been sworn in. Few would have guessed that a freshman Republican congresswoman in the House would have a chance to not only be heard, but get a piece of legislation passed and signed into law by the president that year. However, through sharing a common goal with my colleagues across the aisle, and making the case effectively, I was able to help forge a bipartisan solution to a tragic problem in my district.

The town of Treece in southeast Kansas lies right on the state border. Essentially neighborhoods of the same town, Treece is literally across the street from the town of Picher, OK. In the early 20th century, the area was one of the top zinc and lead producers for World War I and World War II. But after the mining companies left in the 1960s, it became one of the most environmentally devastated areas in the whole country with severe land, air and water pollution. There were huge piles of toxic mining waste, called chat piles, that looked like little mountains and dotted the landscape. There were sinkholes and uncapped mine shafts that would fill with contaminated water, where children would swim and come home with burned–red skin from the acid.

The regional EPA office in Oklahoma bought out and shut down Picher, relocating all the families there. But because they were on the other side of an invisible state line, the families living on the Kansas side of the community were left there and spent years fighting through all sorts of bureaucratic red tape.

A Democrat in the state legislature, Doug Gatewood, brought the issue to my attention during my first month in office. I invited EPA officials to go down and see the contamination and destruction with their own eyes. It really was a sight to behold! After a little convincing, we were able to work together, and then, along with my two Republican colleagues in the Senate at the time – Sam Brownback, now the Kansas governor, and current U.S. Senator Pat Roberts – we pushed legislation through the Democratic-controlled House and Senate to relocate 66 families who owned homes and about a dozen renters. In 2012, the town of Treece was officially disincorporated and removed from the map.

It may not sound like good news, but without the buyout these families would have been forced to remain stuck in a toxic wasteland. The story of Treece is a great example of how we really can overcome partisan divides in Washington if we work together in a collaborative way toward a common goal. The way to do that is to put people before politics and communicate effectively. Even when Democrats controlled everything in Washington, three Republicans were able to get something done. People at home don't believe that's possible in today's environment. But if we look past the politics and put people first, it is.

NO LABELS VOICES
REP. KURT SCHRADER (D-OR)

I learned several important lessons about coming together around shared goals during my years in the Oregon state legislature.

As the Democratic co-chair of the Ways and Means Committee, which had total control of all the dollars spent, I was a common target. The Republican leader in the state senate, Ted Ferrioli, was an especially staunch adversary, always doing his best to undermine what I was doing.

Except one time. There'd been talk of starting a four-year veterinary college for Oregon. As the only veterinarian in the legislature in 2001, I was approached about this and was very inclined to try to make it happen even though money was tight. Since Ted represented a huge swath of agricultural Oregon that was very interested in a functioning veterinary school, I reached out to him. Even though we battled all the time on just about everything, he decided he'd work with me. We gave speeches together on the benefits – I would talk about the small animal and equine end; he'd talk about the livestock end of things. As a result of our coalition, we had overwhelming bipartisan support and the college came to pass.

That partnership helped smooth the way as we moved forward. I had a little more credibility with Ted and frankly, he had a little more credibility with me. We were able to work on some of the difficult budget issues that came along with a little less rhetoric and a little more cooperation. You start to build that slow but sure credibility that is all too lacking in many legislative bodies, particularly in Washington.

In another case, I helped broker a compromise between animal rights activists and the livestock community over the question of what to do with dogs who were chasing, and in some cases injuring or killing, livestock. Both sides shared the goal of keeping the animals safe, so we came up with a solution to move the dogs to a different non-rural setting rather than put them down, and that agreement became law.

On a bigger stage, finding common objectives that will lead to a national strategy will take a lot of listening and extreme political courage. But if we can start to coalesce around common goals, admittedly at a 30,000-foot level, that's a first step in helping us define what we agree on, not what we disagree on, and find common ground.

WORKING TOGETHER
CAN WORK AGAIN:
THE CLINTON AND REAGAN EXAMPLES

BY DR. BILL GALSTON

SENIOR FELLOW, THE BROOKINGS INSTITUTION

> *When it comes to politics and public policy, Bill Galston is one of America's top experts. He's served in the White House, authored eight books, and been a part of six different presidential campaigns. As a Senior Fellow at the Brookings Institution, he's used his experience to help address some of America's toughest challenges. He's also a No Labels co-founder – and strong proponent of a national strategic agenda. In this chapter, he argues that this approach isn't just an abstract theory. It's worked many times in the past. Again and again, even when Washington has been bitterly divided, policymakers have been able to work together to accomplish a common goal.*
>
> *— Jon*

Enduring policy change in the United States comes about in one of two ways. Sometimes one party is so dominant that it can enact its agenda on its own, regardless of what the other party wants. That's what happened during the early years of the New Deal, for instance, and in the first two years of LBJ's Great Society. But moments like these are rare. More typically, one party enjoys a narrow edge over the other rather than a supermajority, and the parties often divide control between the two houses of Congress or between the legislative and executive branches. In such cases, it becomes necessary to build support across party

37

lines before policymakers can achieve lasting progress.

When the parties can agree on goals, the path to agreement on policies becomes smoother. This was true for Ronald Reagan and Tip O'Neill. It was true for Bill Clinton and Newt Gingrich. And it remains true today.

PRESIDENT CLINTON AND SPEAKER GINGRICH

On September 5, 2012, President Bill Clinton stood before the Democratic National Convention in Charlotte, NC. Amid roaring applause, the former president told the crowd, "people ask me all the time how we got four surplus budgets in a row … I always give a one-word answer: Arithmetic."

That's part of the story. Yes, Clinton led the country to its first balanced budget in almost thirty years.[4] But he didn't do it alone. A balanced budget was only possible because the two parties came to agree on that goal and then found a way to reach it together.

This might sound surprising. After all, the Clinton years are often remembered as an unending succession of partisan battles. But in fact, the parties came together more than once to achieve historic agreements – among them, the deal that finally balanced the budget.

For many decades, the Democratic and Republican parties have clashed over levels of taxing and spending, and both parties have displayed ambivalence about balancing the budget when it conflicted with what they regarded as higher priorities. That helps explain why we have so seldom achieved balance.

When Bill Clinton became president, the economy was struggling to emerge from recession, and the budget deficit was large by historical standards. In early 1993, he resolved a debate within his administration by choosing fiscal restraint over expansive public investment, an approach that reduced the deficit without eliminating it.

In the 1994 midterm elections, Newt Gingrich led the

---

4 www.politifact.com/new-jersey/statements/2012/jun/08/bill-clinton/bill-clinton-touts-fiscal-record-president-during-/

Republican Party to a majority in the House for the first time in 40 years. The party's Contract With America featured a balanced budget as a prominent goal.

At first, President Clinton and most members of his party balked. The cuts would be too deep, they said. It wasn't possible in such a short time frame. In February 1995, Clinton released a budget that projected annual deficits of nearly $200 billion through 2005.

Just four months later, Clinton reversed course. In a speech from the Oval Office in June 1995, he endorsed the goal of balanced federal budget and laid out his ideas for reaching it in the way that he believed would best promote the well-being of the people. He insisted that Medicare, Medicaid, and programs to improve education and the environment must be protected from major cuts. "There are fundamental differences between Democrats and Republicans about how to balance the budget," he said. "But this debate must go beyond partisanship. It must be about what's good for America and which approach is more likely to bring prosperity and security to our people over the long run."

With those words, Clinton reframed the conversation in Washington. At that moment, the parties stopped fighting over whether they wanted to balance the budget. Instead, they started debating the best way to get it done.

The period that came next is often remembered for a partisan battle that ended in a government shutdown. But neither party lost sight of the goal of a balanced budget. When Clinton addressed the nation in the midst of the shutdown, he mentioned the importance of balancing the budget more than ten times. For his part, Speaker Gingrich repeatedly underscored his party's commitment to balancing the budget. They disagreed over how quickly the budget could be balanced and what needed to be cut – but they never strayed from that goal.

In the end, of course, the government reopened. The next year Congress passed the Balanced Budget Act of 1997, and Clinton gladly signed it into law. With that law in place – and with rapid growth driving the economy – the United States balanced its budget for the first time in decades and did so for four years in a row.

PRESIDENT REAGAN AND SPEAKER O'NEILL

People sometimes say that Ronald Reagan and Tip O'Neill were able to work together because of their famous agreement that politics should stop at 6 p.m. When Reagan called the speaker, he was known to ask, "Tip, is it after six o'clock?" Then the real conversation would begin.

This cordial relationship was surely important to the successes O'Neill and Reagan shared. But good manners only got them so far. They disagreed on a host of issues ranging from the size of government to foreign policy – and they fought over them. But when they could agree on a goal, they often found a way to get there together.

Take tax reform. They may have disagreed on many of the specific points, but they agreed that America needed a simpler, fairer tax code. Once they had agreed on that goal, it was just a matter of finding a way to get there.

They found that way forward in 1986, when the President and the Speaker built a bipartisan coalition to enact one of the most comprehensive tax reforms in American history. Of course, both sides had to give ground to get there. The Democrats agreed to drop the top tax rate from 50 percent to 28 percent, while Reagan agreed to raise the capital gains tax from 20 percent to 28 percent. The number of tax brackets was reduced. Despite the forces of countless lobbyists, both sides agreed to strike a number of tax deductions that benefited only the rich and the well-connected while failing to promote economic growth. In the end, America had a better, fairer, simpler tax code – and the American people were the winners.

The politics surrounding this issue were just as thorny thirty years ago as they are today. The crucial difference was real commitment by leaders on both sides of the partisan divide to achieve this goal together.

In both of these cases, presidents and congressional leaders found ways to work together across party lines. They can do that again today – and they must. Because while we remain stalled, our competitors won't be standing still, and the next generation of Americans will pay the price.

When President Clinton addressed the nation from the Oval Office that crucial day in 1995, he closed by saying,

> "There are those who have suggested that it might actually benefit one side or the other politically if we had gridlock and ended this fiscal year without a budget. But that would be bad for our country, and we have to do everything we can to avoid it. If we'll just do what's best for our children, our future, and our Nation, and forget about who gets the political advantage, we won't go wrong."

That same spirit should guide us today.

NO LABELS VOICES
REP. CHARLIE DENT (R-PA)

Around Washington, it sometimes feels like we're engaged in trench warfare. Too many seek safety and security in their own trenches – especially if their general re-election seems a sure thing – and no one wants to get out and venture into "no man's land."

The government shutdown of 2013 was a prime example. We were in a situation of terrible division that led to complete dysfunction, with the leaders on both sides unable to reach an agreement. The leadership vacuum provided an opportunity for members like me to step in, try to come up with reasonable solutions and get to "yes."

Right after the shutdown, Rep. Ron Kind and I came together – a Democrat and a Republican – and forged a very simple proposal to reopen the government: pass a continuing resolution for six months, repeal the medical device tax and pay for it with a pension-smoothing provision that was largely agreed to by both sides. We were able to get a critical bipartisan mass in the House to back us and it really caught on. Our common goal was simple: We shared a very strong sense of governance. It was that basic. We all felt that members of Congress have a basic fundamental responsibility to affirmatively govern the nation and fulfill our most basic functions – funding the government and passing a budget.

The leadership, of course, did not embrace this proposal. But to me it really represented the starting point for the negotiations that helped us break the impasse, reopen the government, and make sure the country did not default on its obligations. The fact that we introduced this proposal into the discussion helped us move off the dime – and it became central to the negotiations. Senators Susan Collins and Joe Manchin carried our proposal aggressively in the Senate.

Though there was a lot of leadership opposition to our proposal, there was considerable rank and file support. To me, that represented a glimmer of hope. There are plenty of members on both sides of the aisle who want to get beyond this trench warfare. It will require members of Congress who are not afraid to step out of their comfort zones and who are prepared to deal with a backlash for participating in a consensus-driven process for the good of the country.

NO LABELS VOICES
REP. PETER WELCH (D-VT)

Before entering Congress, I was the Senate president in the Vermont legislature. We had a big Democratic majority, but the governor at the time, Jim Douglas, was a Republican.

In 2005, the Democrats passed a controversial bill that would have extended health care to many people in Vermont. I wanted to expand access to health care, but Governor Douglas was concerned about controlling health care costs, so he vetoed it.

But we didn't walk away from the table and play the blame

game. The governor and I sat down together and we recognized that Republican concerns about cost and Democratic concerns about access *both* had merit. So we incorporated our mutual and legitimate concerns into a common goal: access to health care delivered in an affordable and sustainable way. The next year, we passed a bipartisan bill that has served Vermonters well.

Progress takes effort. And it requires political engagement and mutual respect to work through a tough process with conflicting priorities so you can explain to supporters and adversaries that what you are doing will actually advance a shared goal. That's the hard work of legislating in which all legislators should be engaged.

In Congress, I've found similar ways of making progress by emphasizing areas of agreement rather than conflict. For instance, the Republicans generally haven't agreed with Democratic objectives on climate change, and there continues to be a lot of debate about the science of climate change. But I've found that many Republicans are totally in agreement with Democrats about the benefits of energy efficiency – creating jobs and saving money. So I worked with Republicans like Cory Gardner of Colorado, now a senator, on cutting energy use in federal buildings and with David McKinley of West Virginia on encouraging homeowners to retrofit their homes.

There's immense potential in partnerships with Republicans on practical, common-sense energy efficiency measures. It's a space where people with different points of view can get something done that's good for the country and, just by making progress together, good for Congress.

One of the highest principles all of us claim is a commitment to getting things done for our country. So how do we do that? Like we do in Vermont, let's focus on the things we can agree on, not just the differences between us. It's an old fashioned way of working together that we must restore in Congress.

HERE'S *HOW*: OUR STRATEGY FOR A STRONGER AMERICA THROUGH A NATIONAL STRATEGIC AGENDA

If you've read this far, one thing should be clear above all: Our country doesn't move forward by fighting. We move forward when we have a shared sense of where we need to go. As you've already heard, presidents like Dwight D. Eisenhower, John F. Kennedy, Ronald Reagan, and Bill Clinton all proved this in their times. We should summon that same kind of national aspiration today.

Our challenges today are no larger than those faced by past leaders. Our skills and resources are just as abundant. What we lack today is not the ability; it's the sense of urgency and largely, the sense that we have a common goal we can achieve together. Today, we need objectives to rally around as a nation. We need to identify our most foundational problems and focus the thrust of our energies and our talents on solving them. In this chapter, No Labels identifies those foundational problems and the goals we need to start pursuing today to make our nation stronger tomorrow.

— Joe and Jon

As we were writing this book, we gathered input from experts of every field and every point of view. We asked them all the same questions: What are the most pressing problems our country faces? What are our greatest strengths and most persistent weaknesses? What should the United States be striving toward today?

We also asked the American people the same questions. We conducted a poll where we asked more than a thousand

Americans what our government should be focused on right now. The options ranged from implementing congressional term limits by 2020, to landing humans on Mars by 2035, to everything in between. But ultimately, four major concerns rose to the top for Democrats, Republicans, and independents alike.

Right now the American people are worried about the precarious, fluctuating state of the job market and our sometimes sluggish economic growth. They worry about Medicare, Social Security, and the strength – and sustainability – of our entitlement system. They worry about our government's deficits and long-term fiscal health. And they're concerned about our energy security, and the way our energy policy – or lack of one – positions us to create jobs and compete in the future.

On each of these issues, the experts and the American people agree. These are the big, foundational challenges that we need to confront. They aren't our only national goals – nor should they be. In their poll responses, the American people made it clear that we need to revitalize our infrastructure, support innovation, and do much more to secure our future for the next generation. They said we need to address education and health care, tax reform and poverty. But first, they want us to tackle our most immediate challenges.

This approach makes sense. Because if we solve our biggest, most fundamental challenges today, then we'll be in a much stronger position to tackle every other challenge that we face. We would essentially build a runway from which our national ambitions could take flight.

To that end, we're proposing four essential goals that require our urgent effort.

1. Create 25 million net new jobs over the next 10 years.
2. Secure Medicare and Social Security for another 75 years.
3. Balance the federal budget by 2030.
4. Make America energy secure by 2024.

Each of these objectives has been on the table, in one form

or another, for many years, but very little progress has been made with any of them. It's not because the solutions aren't clear, but because we haven't focused our talents and resources. That's precisely why the process of setting clear goals is so important. It's the only way to start a process that transforms empty rhetoric into decisive action.

It's one thing for politicians to offer vague talk about "fiscal responsibility" or "energy security." It will be entirely different if they sign onto clear goals with clear measures of success and failure. If both sides buy into a set of shared objectives, it will be possible for the American people to judge the progress that their government makes each year. If something isn't working, our leaders will be able to refine their course to get closer to these ends. And most importantly, it will be possible for the voters to hold leaders accountable if they aren't working together to get our country where they've all agreed it needs to go.

In the pages ahead, we'll discuss these goals one at a time. We'll offer our thoughts on why they are urgent today, why they will make us stronger tomorrow, and why we should be able to achieve each one. With all of these challenges, the solutions are out there. We just need our political leaders to work together to figure out how to get it done.

CREATE 25 MILLION NET NEW JOBS OVER THE NEXT 10 YEARS

When James Truslow Adams coined the phrase "The American Dream" in 1931, the ideas he inspired were truly radical.

He saw America as a land that was different from Europe for one very important, very unique reason. In America, who you are is defined not by the nobility of your blood, but by your commitment to hard work.

"The American Dream," Adams said, "is that dream of a land in which life should be better and richer and fuller for everyone, with opportunity for each according to ability or achievement."

Well, a lot has changed since 1931.

For one thing, a recent Gallup study revealed that people don't want the same things they used to. The desire for money, love, and freedom used to top the lists of aspirations worldwide.

But now, everyone wants the same thing: a good job.[5] And it makes sense, because money, love, and freedom are all connected to having a good job. A job means the ability to support your family. It means the freedom to live as you choose. A job, above all, is the pathway to the American dream.

Unfortunately, since the most recent recession, a job is also one thing that's become much too hard to come by.

The Great Recession cost our country millions of jobs.[6] Countless Americans watched as loved ones lost their dignity and their ability to support their families. Of the Americans who were able to find work, more than half were forced to settle for lower paying positions.[7] Though the economy has rebounded in the more than five years since the official end of the Great Recession, there are still pockets of America, and entire industries, with high unemployment. What's more, the economy hasn't added the roughly 10 million jobs needed to keep up with growth in the working-age population.[8]

This is why creating jobs needs to be a top priority for our elected leaders. And that's why we're calling on our leaders to rally around a crucial goal: to create 25 million jobs over the next decade.

This isn't a pipe dream – in fact, there's already some cause for optimism. In the spring of 2015, the unemployment rate dropped to a near seven-year low of 5.4 percent, signs of real

---

5   businessjournal.gallup.com/content/151865/entrepreneurs-save-america.aspx#1

6   money.cnn.com/2010/07/02/news/economy/jobs_gone_forever/

7   www.thefiscaltimes.com/Articles/2013/02/07/Great-Recession-Leaves-Long-Lasting-Scars-Poll#sthash.IDDKUfiT.dpuf

8   www.nytimes.com/interactive/2014/06/05/upshot/how-the-recession-reshaped-the-economy-in-255-charts.html?_r=0&abt=0002&abg=1

momentum.[9] Experts expect job growth to continue steadily over the next decade. The manufacturing sector has seen consistent growth,[10] Americans are buying more homes, and CEOs around the country predict more economic expansion.[11]

We're heading in the right direction, but we could still veer off course at any time. Just look at what happened when our leaders shut down the government in October 2013. In the end, those political theatrics cost our country 120,000 jobs.[12]

Instead of this brand of dangerous gridlock, we need a simple commitment from Washington. No more self-inflicted economic wounds. Instead, leaders from both sides of the aisle need to recommit our country to job creation. That could mean investing in repairing America's infrastructure. It could mean streamlining regulations to help new and small businesses hire. There is no shortage of great ideas. Right now, there's simply a shortage of political commitment to turn those ideas into reality.

Ultimately, most Americans want the same basic things. They want good jobs. They want to go to work every day, provide for their families, and leave their children a better world than the one they found.

Over the next ten years, creating 25 million jobs can restore 25 million hopes, 25 million opportunities, and 25 million American dreams. This is a goal we all need to pursue.

SECURE MEDICARE AND SOCIAL
SECURITY FOR ANOTHER 75 YEARS

It's 1940.

Social Security was founded four years ago, and Ida May

---

9 www.newsweek.com/us-employment-drops-near-seven-year-low-329923

10 www.npr.org/blogs/thetwo-way/2013/12/06/249224096/203k-jobs-added-in-november-u-s-unemployment-at-7-percent

11 www.voanews.com/content/us-ceos-slightly-more-optimistic-about-economy/1803530.html

12 www.csmonitor.com/Business/Donald-Marron/2013/1024/The-government-shutdown-cost-the-US-120-000-jobs

Fuller is the first person to receive Social Security benefits. It's a time when payroll taxes are low, 42 workers share the cost for every one retiree, and the retirement age is higher than life expectancy.[13] Ida May lives to be 100 years old, and she counts on Social Security benefits every single month for 35 years.[14]

It's 1965.

Congress and the president have come together to create a new program: Medicare. Now, Americans over the age of 65 can retire securely and safely, without having to worry that they won't be able to get the medical care that they need.

It's 2015.

People are living longer, depending on Social Security and Medicare more than ever before. Life expectancy exceeds retirement by more than a decade, and 75 million baby boomers populate the planet.[15] The elderly make up a greater and greater percentage of the United States population, making entitlements even more unstable. In 1944, there were 42 workers for every retiree. Today, that number has shrunk to 3. The system is becoming less sustainable every day – yet Washington doesn't seem ready to act.[16]

It's 2033.

One billion people on the planet are over the age of retirement. For the first time in global history, the number of people over 65 exceeds the number of children under the age of five.[17] One out of every five Americans is over the age of 65, and the Social Security trust fund is now insolvent. That means Social Security can only provide 75 percent of promised

13 www.ssa.gov/history/lifeexpect.html

14 www.greatwatersfinancial.com/files/64179/MNgoodAge_
skipGWF.pdf

15 www.pewresearch.org/fact-tank/2015/01/16/this-year-
millennials-will-overtake-baby-boomers/

16 www.usatoday.com/story/opinion/2013/10/21/obamacare-
medicare-affordable-care-act-column/3145983/

17 www.aarp.org/content/dam/aarp/livable-communities/learn/
demographics/the-future-of-a-generation-how-new-americans-
will-help-support-retiring-baby-boomers-aarp.pdf

benefits to the people who need it and have earned it. Meanwhile, Medicare became insolvent in 2026.[18]

As more and more Americans expect to live *longer*, the very systems set up to ensure that they live *better* struggle to survive. After years of hard work, too many Americans retire under a shadow of stress. Ida May Fuller becomes a symbol of a broken promise and a failed system.

That's where we're headed if we don't change course and reform these programs soon. There's no reason to wait – we should get this done right away.

As America's population ages, we'll only need Social Security and Medicare more. Today, fewer than half of American households ages 55 to 64 have saved enough to retire on.[19] Already, the majority of Americans over 65 get two-thirds of their income from Social Security.[20] Our country's retirees literally can't afford to lose out on the benefits they have paid into.

For the last half century, we've made a sacred promise to our citizens. In exchange for a life of hard work, your secure retirement is guaranteed. But that promise is about to reach its expiration date, unless Washington takes action.

It's not that we don't know what to do. In fact, many experts – in and out of government – have come up with ways to keep these systems secure for generations far into the future. Washington isn't lacking a way; but increasingly, it seems to be lacking the will. Part of that is a function of politics – the fear, on both sides, that their opponents will use the popularity of these programs as a bludgeon against any meaningful steps toward reform. But largely, the failure to act is not rooted in fear; it's rooted in complacency, in the belief that these problems will be solved someday by somebody else. That kind of logic has

---

18 www.politico.com/story/2013/05/medicare-exhausted-2026-trustees-92066.html#ixzz2nH8KMPHU

19 www.nytimes.com/2013/03/31/opinion/sunday/social-security-present-and-future.html

20 www.nytimes.com/2013/03/31/opinion/sunday/social-security-present-and-future.html

put this problem off for too long; and now, we are genuinely running out of time.

That's why we're setting a goal: Secure Medicare and Social Security for another 75 years.

Washington has to rid itself of the habit of kicking questions about entitlements down the road. This is a chance to secure these vital programs for generations. It's a chance to ensure that the children being born today can live with a certain promise that they will receive the benefits they earn. Social Security and Medicare are two of the most important programs the U.S. government has ever created; it's time to restore Americans' confidence in these vital parts of American life.

BALANCE THE FEDERAL BUDGET BY 2030

"This budget marks the end of an era. An end to decades of deficits that have shackled our economy, paralyzed our politics and held our people back."

With those words, President Bill Clinton put a ribbon on a historic moment. It was a gift to the American people: a balanced budget for the first time in 30 years. As Bill Galston discussed in the previous chapter, our leaders in Washington achieved this monumental accomplishment by working together.

In the 1990s, President Clinton and Speaker Gingrich put their differences aside long enough to turn urgent red ink into a triumphant black zero.[21] And hopes were high at the start of the new millennium, as the Congressional Budget Office projected more surpluses to come.

But then, things started to take a turn for the worse. Starting in 2002, we began running budget deficits again – and the deficit exploded to over a trillion dollars in the years that followed.

Recently, we've seen a partial – and welcome – reversal of this trend. At the end of the 2013 fiscal year, the federal deficit

21 www.nytimes.com/1998/02/03/us/clinton-budget-overview-president-offers-first-budget-balance-nearly-30-years.html?pagewanted=all&src=pm

fell by 37 percent. For the first time since the financial collapse of 2008, the deficit sat below a trillion dollars.[22] Our economy is getting stronger, and our government is spending less.

But the Congressional Budget Office projects the deficit will begin to rise again in 2018, reaching $1 trillion by 2025.[23] It's not at all clear what our leaders plan to do about that or how they plan to balance the budget. Politicians from both sides of the aisle do plenty of talk about the deficit. They're eager to pelt the American people with dire predictions, and they're more than happy to tell you who to blame for them. But it's time for them to stop simply talking about the budget and get to work balancing it.

Again, there's no undiscovered secret about how to get this done. Economists across the board agree on ways to balance the budget. Ways that are both fiscally responsible and socially accountable. But these options don't matter if we can't get our leaders in Washington in the same room to talk about them.

Balancing the budget by 2030 wouldn't just be the chance for Washington to make history again. It would be the opportunity to revitalize our economy. It would be the possibility to give generations to come a truly worthy gift: not just a balanced budget, but a sustainable future.

MAKE AMERICA ENERGY SECURE BY 2024

What if we told you that right now, America has the chance to create jobs, spur economic growth, protect the environment, *and* strengthen our national security?

It might sound too good to be true – but it's not a fantasy. Just consider these facts:

Right now, the energy sector has the potential to grow much more quickly than almost every other part of the economy. Over the next few years, the domestic oil and gas industries alone are projected to grow over four times faster than the rest of the

---

22 www.washingtonpost.com/blogs/wonkblog/wp/2013/10/30/
    congratulations-america-your-deficit-fell-37-percent-in-2013/
23 https://www.cbo.gov/publication/49973

economy.[24] Citigroup recently estimated that if we can secure an abundant supply of energy here at home, our real GDP could increase by as much as 3.3 percent. That might not sound like much, but it would mean hundreds of billions of dollars added to our GDP – and as many as 3.6 million new jobs.[25]

This kind of growth could transform our economy. It could kick start a whole new wave of job creation, because for every American job created in the oil and natural gas industries, three more jobs are created in other sectors across our economy.[26] So today, the opportunity is clear. We have the chance to revitalize our economy with jobs ranging from hydraulic engineering, to installing solar panels, to developing the next great innovation in renewable energy. Research today could lead to the idea that powers our cars, heats our homes, and changes all of our lives for decades and even centuries to come.

A coherent energy strategy could unlock all this – but first we need to take advantage of this opportunity.

The good news is that we've already started producing a lot more energy at home in recent years. Today, only 27 percent of the oil we use is imported[27] – a major improvement over the peak of 60 percent we hit in 2005.[28] But that still leaves us relying on foreign nations for a considerable share of our energy supply. As a result, billions of American dollars are flowing into the coffers of countries that, to put it lightly, haven't exactly been our best friends in the past.

If we want to change America's energy future, then we need decisive leadership and an effective energy policy. We need a policy that taps more into our existing energy supply, while

24 reports.weforum.org/energy-for-economic-growth-energy-vision-update-2012/#chapter-the-role-of-the-energy-sector-in-job-creation

25 www.businessinsider.com/a-spike-in-us-oil-production-is-about-to-make-it-the-new-middle-east-2012-3

26 reports.weforum.org/energy-for-economic-growth-energy-vision-update-2012/#chapter-the-role-of-the-energy-sector-in-job-creation

27 http://www.eia.gov/tools/faqs/faq.cfm?id=727&t=6

28 articles.latimes.com/2011/oct/29/business/la-fi-oil-boom-20111029

spurring the innovation we need to create viable alternative energy sources.

If we don't create a coherent strategy that allows us to satisfy our energy demands at home, we'll always be left looking beyond our borders for help. That would be an enormous missed economic opportunity – an unforced error that we just can't afford.

This isn't rocket science. Politicians from both sides of the aisle agree that we need to take greater strides towards energy self-sufficiency. That's why we're proposing a new goal for our nation. We need to achieve energy security by 2024. And there's no reason that we shouldn't be able to achieve it.

Policy wonks have already outlined the basic requirements needed to make the transition. If our political leaders from both parties can agree to make this a priority, we know we can get it done. This is a straightforward, common sense, manageable goal – we just need the political will to reach it at last.

THIS CAN BE DONE

To be sure, there's a lot more we need to do as a country. This is far from an exhaustive list of all the challenges America faces in this century and beyond. But this is the first step – a set of mutually reinforcing objectives that will push us forward to a stronger future where we can achieve much, much more.

There will be a lot of tough decisions ahead. Accomplishing any of this is going to require real tradeoffs, and no one is going to get everything sought.

In this book, however, we have purposely stopped short of suggesting *which* tradeoffs will be needed. That's the mistake that is made too commonly in our political debates. Too often, political actors start parsing the smallest policy disagreements right from the beginning – before they've ever agreed on what they're actually trying to achieve. Before long, they're completely divided – and all because they got wrapped up in the details before they took the time to build consensus around the big picture.

This book is the first step toward remedying that problem. It's the start of a campaign to change the conversation – and the mindset – in Washington. It might take an election or two before we see the total shift – but ultimately, we need our elected leaders to start reorienting our government toward problem solving.

It won't be easy – but real leadership demands that you reconcile opposing forces and different points of view. That's what we need for the good of our country right now. Because the solutions are out there – and now it's up to our leaders to get together and work out precisely what to do.

We want the idea of problem solving through common objectives to become part of the presidential campaign. It will be game changing. We are imploring the next president to start his or her administration with a clear commitment to building consensus around shared goals. We expect the president-elect to meet with the opposition even before being sworn in. And on January 20, 2017, the new president can then use his or her inaugural address to tell the country that the two parties have met and have agreed on goals and steps to achieve them. This is how we can make our country stronger.

We are also asking the next president to meet with leaders of both parties within the first 30 days in office to select one or more of the four goals to pursue together in earnest. Any presidential candidate who commits to taking this action will earn the No Labels Problem Solver Seal of Approval on the eve of New Hampshire primary voting. (See next chapter for more details.) With so many candidates in the ring, we hope to be handing out a lot of seals!

It may be easy to look at the scope of our problems – and the boldness of these goals – and think this can't be done. But it can be. Washington has come together many times in the past, often when our challenges were more severe, and our divisions more stark. We can do it again. We *must* do it again.

THE NO LABELS SEAL OF APPROVAL: ELECTING A PROBLEM-SOLVER PRESIDENT IN 2016

BY NO LABELS CO-FOUNDERS

What do we expect to be hearing during this campaign season? If it's like past elections, we'll hear lots of rhetoric, sound bites, empty promises, partisan jabs. The American people have become so inured to the largely meaningless discourse of election years that we no longer expect – or demand from our candidates – serious discussions or commitments for bold action.

We intend to change all that, beginning this election cycle.

The No Labels Problem Solver Seal of Approval, which we awarded to congressional candidates who embraced a problem-solving platform in the 2014 election, has proven to be a potent electoral weapon.

This campaign season, we believe it can help elect the kind of president nearly all Americans say they want: a problem-solving president.

Sometime before the New Hampshire primary, No Labels will be awarding its Problem Solvers Seal to any and all presidential candidates – Democrat, Republican, independent or other; we want them all! – who commit to a framework for bipartisan problem solving through a National Strategic Agenda that sets out goals for this country.

We will be lending our muscle to presidential candidates who embrace the idea that as a nation with an evenly divided government, we are better served when leaders of both parties identify big priorities and goals *together* and then work within a bipartisan, problem-solving framework to achieve those goals.

We are not just asking the candidates to talk a good game. Talking about working together, bipartisan goals, being a uniter, not a divider, etc., is easy. We hear that again and again and know it rarely translates to progress. We're asking for something more. We want a commitment. We're demanding accountability. And we're looking for action – very specific action – in exchange for our support.

To earn the Problem Solver Seal in January, 2016, which we believe will provide a competitive edge in the primaries especially where independents can cast votes, a presidential candidate must take these steps:

1. **Support the notion that America needs a National Strategic Agenda based on the four goals we've identified that enjoy majority support across partisan and ideological lines.** Those goals are:
   - Create 25 million new jobs over the next 10 years;
   - Secure Medicare and Social Security for another 75 years;
   - Balance the federal budget by 2030;
   - Make America energy secure by 2024

2. **Agree to initiate an effort within the first 30 days of his or her administration to begin work on one or more of the four goals.** This effort must include:
   - Gathering together congressional leaders of both parties and from both chambers to forge agreement on a bipartisan process for making progress on the goal or goals:
   - Forging a robust work plan that includes the assignment of working groups or congressional committees to study the relevant issues; and agreement on timelines and metrics for success

against the respective goal or goals.

3. **Agree to affirm these commitments in public remarks and/or on his or her campaign website.**

This commitment meets the American people's demand for action, not rhetoric. It provides a blueprint for the kind of problem solving and decision making that leads to big, bold achievements, but is absent in Washington today.

Congressional candidates, too, are eligible to earn the No Labels Problem Solver Seal through their support of the House and Senate resolutions calling for a National Strategic Agenda. Any member of Congress who signs onto one of these resolutions will be awarded the seal.

The 2016 election needs to be all about "how" candidates plan to bring our nation together around common goals. We believe the National Strategic Agenda is the answer.

We have seen the impact the Problem Solver Seal has had. Frankly, many politicians underestimated its currency in 2014, not fully appreciating the public's hunger for a saner, more productive approach to politics and government.

In the most publicized – and controversial – case, No Labels awarded the Problem Solver Seal to Rep. Cory Gardner, a Republican from Colorado, who was running for a Senate seat against incumbent Senate Democrat Mark Udall. In this closely watched and hotly contested race last year, No Labels invited both candidates to commit to the No Labels agenda of reaching across the aisle and supporting unifying goals for the country in order to earn our Seal of Approval. Sen. Udall declined the invitation while Rep. Gardner actively embraced it.

Many Democrats were furious that No Labels awarded its Problem Solver Seal to Rep. Gardner, but not Sen. Udall, and accused the organization of taking partisan sides and favoring Republicans. In fact, our support for Rep. Gardner, who ended up defeating Sen. Udall, was consistent with our approach of awarding the seal to any candidate who publicly commits to the No Labels concept of a bipartisan, problem-solving governing process.

We had hoped to award the seal to both contestants in the Colorado race, just as we did in the Iowa Senate race, where we gave the Seal of Approval to both Democratic Rep. Bruce Braley and Republican challenger Joni Ernst.

As more and more voters express their frustration with the dysfunction in Washington and demand something more from their representatives, we expect to see more candidates seeking the Problem Solver Seal to signify their commitment to a new kind of politics.

Since our problem-solving mission resonates so strongly with independent voters, this badge is likely to be especially valuable to candidates in states like New Hampshire, which has a higher percentage of independent voters than either Democrats or Republicans – and which has an open primary election.

At the presidential level, this seal will be a litmus test – a way of showing that the men and women who seek this high office are truly committed to working with their political opponents to solve the nation's most urgent problems, and not just spitting out election year rhetoric and talking points.

We hope all the presidential candidates will see this as an opportunity to reach across the aisle, commit to a new way of doing business in Washington, put the welfare of this country ahead of party politics – and proudly proclaim and promise to voters that they will do whatever it takes to be a true problem-solving leader.

LEAVING THE WORLD
A BETTER PLACE

BY LISA BORDERS

NO LABELS CO-FOUNDER AND VICE CHAIR

There's something very meaningful and personal for me in the principles of inclusion, common ground, and ideological diversity that are at the heart of No Labels' mission and spirit. As an African-American child of the South who grew up in the racially charged 1960s, I look for those values in every one of my pursuits – personal, professional, and political.

My background set the stage for my interests and my life's work. My paternal grandfather was a minister in Atlanta who helped integrate the buses and worked to get the first African Americans hired as police officers. Maynard Jackson, the first black mayor of Atlanta, launched his political career from my grandfather's pulpit.

Coming from a civil rights family, it was no accident that I helped integrate an all-white independent school. My parents, worried that I wasn't challenged in school as a sixth-grader – straight A's in academic subjects and a D in conduct tipped them off – sent me to this private school. I became one of a half-dozen African Americans in a student body of about 1,800. Moving to the new school, I was finally challenged academically – but also socially and emotionally. There wasn't a day between my 7th- and 12th-grade years that I didn't hear the "n-word" tossed my way. Kids were cruel. Like most adolescents, I wanted desperately to fit in, but of course I was perceived as different.

It was a pretty tough time, introducing me to life's hard knocks at a very early age. But it also set the tenor and tone for the rest of my life.

As I live my life today, every time I see a disenfranchised class, whether it's women, people of color, those with disabilities, or those with different sexual orientations, I want to become their champion. It's why I serve as the executive sponsor for the LGBT community at Coca-Cola, where I'm vice president for Global Community Affairs and chair of the Coca-Cola Foundation. I'm following in my grandfather's very large footsteps, trying to ensure everyone has equal access and equal opportunities.

That's why I'm so passionate about No Labels and, specifically, the four important goals for America that are the pillars of the National Strategic Agenda.

Where race was the predominant marker dividing this nation when I was growing up – and still runs like a river through this country, especially in the South – economics is the great divider today, driving a giant wedge between the haves and the have nots.

The No Labels agenda – seeking progress on jobs, the budget, entitlements and energy security – is one that benefits everyone; it is largely built around economic concerns and areas of agreement among those of all political stripes. These are worthy goals the entire country can rally around.

As a former vice mayor of the city of Atlanta, I consistently saw the value and benefit of coming together over shared goals and putting action and progress ahead of politics. When I ran for office in 2004, no one asked if I was a Democrat or a Republican. No one cared if my views tilted to the left or to the right. Voters wanted to know what kind of plan I had for trash pick-ups and what I would do to make sure the streets were safe for their kids.

Once in office, as vice mayor and president of the city council, the same sort of pragmatism was the order of the day. All of the city officials knew we needed to balance our budget. We wanted to make sure the police and fire-fighting forces were fully staffed. We wanted to provide a quality education for our children. These common goals — fundamentals that knit the social fabric of any municipal jurisdiction — drove us to work together, to put the interests of the citizens ahead of any other considerations, to act. There was no room, no time, and no tolerance for petty political games or power trips.

So why not try to bring this pragmatic, rational approach to governance at a higher level? That's where we at No Labels have set our sights. After all, these are goals that the majority of Americans have told us are priorities for them.

Our mantra at No Labels is that, regardless of our political leanings, we as a people have common goals. Frankly, we also have common enemies. We all need to be battling the dubious distinction of being the first generation to leave our society and our planet in worse shape than it was in when we inherited it. No one wants to leave their children the immense burdens that result from poor, irresponsible financial policies, ineffectual leadership, and ongoing political gridlock.

The goals we've outlined in the National Strategic Agenda will not be a panacea. But tackling them together with a strategy and accountability will be major progress and, we expect, a step toward a new culture of problem solving.

This is no pie-in-the-sky, "Pollyanna" shot of sentimentality. This is an action plan, a hard-hitting, pragmatic roadmap for the tough work that our leaders need to take up every day.

It will require buy-in from members of Congress, from the president, and from citizens who must press for this action by telling our elected officials they expect nothing less.

We're not asking anyone to give up their party affiliation or loyalty. We're merely asking our political leaders to think of themselves as problem solvers *before* they think of themselves as a Democrat or Republican.

When our elected officials can stand and say, "I am a problem solver," and take steps to prove it, all of us — of every race, every class, every ideology — will benefit.

I have many reasons to be optimistic. My background, for starters, shows me the power of equal opportunity. My other grandfather, my mother's father, worked for 30 years as a chauffeur at the Coca-Cola Co., the same place I serve today as a vice president. His wife, my grandmother, worked there for 15 years as a maid. My family has gone from the chauffeur's seat to the executive suite in two generations so I know firsthand that America is an amazing place.

I'm also extremely heartened to have been a part of No Labels from the start and to have seen it grow in five short years from a simple, common-sense idea to an influential movement of nearly half a million people. We now have a congressional caucus, citizen leaders in all 435 districts, a forceful presence on the presidential campaign – and an action plan in the form of a National Strategic Agenda that will help us leave the nation in better shape than we found it for the next generation. That's a worthy legacy for all of us.

FROM PARTISAN GULFS
TO BIPARTISAN GOALS

BY CHARLIE BLACK
NO LABELS VICE CHAIR

As someone who spent the first half of his adult life running political campaigns for Republicans, I know a thing or two about stoking partisan fires.

As a lobbyist trying to press Congress to act and accomplish major initiatives, my current work, I know that those same partisan flames often snuff out any chance of legislative action or results.

To accomplish anything of major consequence in Washington, you need a bipartisan coalition. You need political leaders who are willing to work toward that end, no matter how far to the left or the right they may be. And you need goals that both sides agree are worth fighting for.

These days, that problem-solving approach seems to be in short supply. The effect of that shortfall has been a country that appears aimless, with no economic game plan or strategy for the coming years, much less the more distant future.

Like many Americans, I've been frustrated by the ineffectiveness of the federal government to control its own finances and do any long-range planning. I know there's a better, more productive way of governing. I've seen numerous examples over the years of the two parties coming together and negotiating big, game-changing agreements, even in the most politically heated times and even among the most ideologically driven leaders.

In 1997, President Clinton negotiated a balanced budget agreement with two of the most conservative leaders in the history of Congress – House Speaker Newt Gingrich and Senate Leader Trent Lott. They had to sit down and work very hard – and look beyond their vast differences. But with the common goal of a balanced budget, they got it done. Some people forget that in the year 2000 we had a balanced budget because of that agreement.

There are other examples. The education reform bill, No Child Left Behind, now in the process of being updated, was a compromise between President George W. Bush and Senate Democrat Ted Kennedy of Massachusetts. A decade earlier, the Americans with Disabilities Act of 1990 was signed into law by President George H.W. Bush after a long, arduous negotiating process between the Republican president and his GOP colleagues, like Sen. Bob Dole of Kansas, and Democrats like Sen. Kennedy and Sen. Tom Harkin of Iowa.

Even in the current highly polarized environment, we've seen occasional instances of bipartisan problem solving breaking through the gridlock. Vice President Joe Biden and Senate Minority Leader Mitch McConnell managed to broker a budget agreement between President Obama and Congress in 2013. It wasn't exactly smooth sailing, but in the end, we did limit spending some and bring deficits down while giving each side some of their priority needs.

These things can be done. But to make this sort of bipartisan approach more than just an exception to the rule, to help it take root, we desperately need some kind of long-range agreement on goals for this nation. That's where No Labels is playing a significant role. The National Strategic Agenda is built around big, mutually agreed-upon goals – and it is an urgently needed vehicle for progress.

We've seen that even on the small, day-to-day decisions, our elected officials can't reach agreement because partisan politics gets in the way. An independent force out there that isn't beholden to Republicans or Democrats, conservatives or liberals, but instead is devoted to problem solving and the best interest of the American people is critical.

Given the opportunity, most politicians want to solve problems. They want to get things done. Most of them feel it's not only the right thing to do, but it helps them back home to be identified, not as a bomb thrower, but a problem solver. The coalition of Problem Solvers in Congress will only grow. Then it's important to have the next president plugged into the process and committed to the goals.

My hope is that, running into the large and active No Labels groups along the campaign trail, all of the presidential candidates will recognize the hunger among voters for this approach and will declare themselves problem solvers. Then, by the time we have two nominees, each of them will tell the nation that he or she will get together with the bipartisan leadership within the first 30 days in office and start working on the big issues.

These goals are all vitally important to the economy and the future of the country. While not every single member of Congress will agree to all of them, they are big ideas that enjoy the support of a critical mass of legislators and citizens of both parties.

Once our political leaders agree to the goals, it will be easier to sit down and negotiate the details. They'll know they have the support of an influential nonpartisan group that is just looking for solutions and offering a proven strategy for finding them, as well as the backing of a large constituency back home and throughout the country that is rooting for them to succeed.

AMERICA'S TEST:
A NATIONAL STRATEGY
FOR COMPETITIVENESS

BY MICHAEL E. PORTER
HARVARD BUSINESS SCHOOL

As the head of the Institute for Strategy and Competitiveness at Harvard Business School, Michael Porter is one of America's leading authorities in the study of national competitiveness. He has authored numerous books including Competitive Strategy, Competitive Advantage of Nations, On Competition, and Redefining Health Care. In this chapter, Professor Porter argues that America is no longer poised to be the most competitive nation in the 21st century. We need to restore our competitive advantage – and a shared national strategy is the best way to do that.

— Joe

I can't think of a more important priority in America today than defining our shared goals as a nation, and having a national strategy to address them.

Most Americans believe that we are still the most competitive economy. Our prosperity is assumed. We think of our nation as the most productive, innovative, and dynamic, and in some respects we are. Because competitiveness is assumed, the vast majority of attention is focused on social issues.

However, the economic prosperity of the U.S. has been faltering. This began decades ago and our performance began declining in the late 1990s to 2000, well before the Great Recession of 2008. Job generation has slowed down dramatically from previous decades, wages have stagnated or fallen except for the most educated, and the proportion of Americans working has dropped to a 30-year low. The average American is struggling. The American dream is at risk.

Many people believe our current economic difficulties are the result of the Great Recession, and that stimulus will be a solution, rather than confronting the fundamental structural problems we face. Most Americans, especially those with higher incomes, don't realize how serious the threat to our competitiveness actually is.[29]

A competitive economy is one where companies operating in the U.S. can compete successfully in global markets while maintaining and improving the wages and standard of living of the average worker. Shared prosperity is the only way our economy can create economic opportunity for all Americans. Without shared prosperity, it's hard for our economy to grow, businesses will not be able to find the workers they want to hire, and political divisions will produce gridlock.

A competitive economy is not just about economic success, but also what allows us to address all the other things we care about. If the U.S. is not competitive, then America will have trouble meeting all our other goals and aspirations. Our influence in foreign policy, our ability to create fair rules in the international trading system, and our ability to tackle the many social challenges we face will be severely limited if our economy cannot grow, generate good jobs, support rising wages, and expand tax revenues so we can balance the budget. Right now, we're moving in the opposite direction, toward limits on resources and diminished opportunity.

Today's debate is not about competitiveness but on how to divide the pie – who should get more and who's getting too much. We're blaming each other, but the real problem is that the pie is shrinking for a large part of our population.

Competitiveness depends on creating a highly productive

---

29 fortune.com/2015/03/26/a-wake-up-call-for-tomorrows-top-1-percent-rebuild-americas-middle-class/

environment in which to do business, and productive workers with the skills to support good wages. America has allowed its business environment to erode in infrastructure, education, health care costs, complicated regulation and many other areas. Highly skilled citizens are prospering, but the good jobs for the average citizen have been moving offshore where doing business is less costly.

Despite the serious structural problems we face, America lacks any strategy to address them. What is a strategy? A strategy is an integrated set of steps to meet an important goal. A strategy for competitiveness would address the most important and pressing challenges facing the U.S. economy – from balancing the budget, to bringing our corporate tax system in line with other leading nations, to improving mid-level skills – as well as the steps needed to take advantage of our most important economic opportunities like our new competitive advantage in energy.

Strategy involves making choices and setting priorities, not trying to please every constituency or tackle every issue. A strategy is about getting things done, not holding out to get everything on the wish list of every constituency. Once you have a strategy, it becomes the framework against which to test every investment, policy, and bill in Congress. The legislation that should be moved quickly through Congress is that which addresses our core strategic agenda.

The United States is unusual in not having a national strategy. As one who works with leaders all around the world, I can tell you that most nations have one. They set explicit economic goals and create an agenda for achieving them. In South Korea, for instance, leaders have been very strategic about the steps required to move the country to a higher level of skill and technology, which is needed to raise the income level in what has been an upper middle income country. South Korea is now a highly sophisticated economy with leading global firms such as Samsung, an increasingly efficient business environment, and a growing pool of highly educated people.

If we look back over the last century, America has set

bold agendas as a nation: universal public education, land grant universities, the interstate highway system, a commitment to open competition and strict antitrust, the National Science Foundation, sending a man to the moon, creating the Internet, and others. These bold agendas and others built critical national economic assets that enabled America to be competitive.

In the early 1980s, when Japan was recognized as a serious challenge, we came together as a nation to do some deep soul searching about what America needed to do about it. President Reagan appointed a bipartisan Presidential Commission on U.S. Competitiveness, and important progress took place both in government and the private sector.

Today, we face a far greater challenge than the one we faced from Japan. Part of the challenge comes from the fact that many other nations have raised the bar – better education and skills of their citizens, reduced corruption and government intervention, and rapidly improving business environments.

But, our greatest challenge is not from other countries, but from within. America has made little progress in a decade on any of the economic policy steps that we know are critical. We have allowed our business environment to erode, the costs of doing business to go up, and the skills of the average American to slip behind. We need to act now so we can get things done, before it's too late.

I think most Americans are beginning to intuitively understand that we need a plan – and that we don't have one. There is a lot of talk in Washington, but everyone is talking past each other and not getting anything done. America is not organized or inclined to be very strategic. We tend to approach things issue by issue. We don't get together to say, "Given all our issues, which are the ones we need to focus on now?"

To develop a competitiveness strategy for America, we need to be brutally realistic about our challenges. Yet right now, political speech is incapable of these kinds of assessments. Instead, we lapse into "feel good" rhetoric, while each party or interest group sees its pet issues as the only priorities.

That needs to change, because the campaign for American

competitiveness is the most important campaign that will be run in America during this era in our history. We have to win this campaign. If we don't, there will be more "have nots," more inequality, and the nation will turn against itself.

I'm still optimistic, because America retains crucial and distinctive competitive strengths – like our entrepreneurial climate, innovative culture, and great universities. With smart and committed leadership, a new strategy for shared prosperity is possible. This possibility starts with having the right ideas. It starts with a new shared understanding of what we mean by competitiveness, who is affected, what is at stake, where we stand, and how we need to move forward. Once the majority of Americans understands that the shared goal of competitiveness and a plan to get there are essential, we will see real progress.

For our political leaders, being strategic will require a very different concept for governing. For we citizens, it will require choosing and evaluating our political leaders based on whether they can accomplish the essential steps necessary for our nation to prosper.

I am hopeful that No Labels, with its focus on bipartisan solutions, can help frame the challenge facing America today in a way that our political dialogue has failed to do – and help create a consensus on a national strategy for competitiveness.

NO LABELS VOICES
GLENN HUBBARD
DEAN OF COLUMBIA BUSINESS SCHOOL AND FORMER CHAIRMAN OF THE COUNCIL OF ECONOMIC ADVISERS

In February of 2001, President George W. Bush stood before a joint session of Congress and laid out his vision for the country.

It was a divisive moment in our nation's history. The year before had seen a bitterly contested election followed by an even more contentious recount in Florida. But now that he was in office, President Bush was calling for a major tax overhaul. "To create economic growth and opportunity," he said, "we must put money back into the hands of the people who buy goods and create jobs."[30]

The moment seemed ripe for another all-out partisan battle. Yet despite the ill-will remaining from the election on both sides, President Bush's plan ultimately received bipartisan support. Democrats in both houses of Congress got behind the proposal – and Democratic Senator Max Baucus, who later became Chairman of the Finance Committee – helped write the tax reform package that Bush ultimately signed.

How did President Bush forge this unity of purpose in a time of division? The answer was simple: Both sides saw a clear goal.

At the time of the president's speech to Congress, the U.S. economy was in bad shape. While economic growth slowed, unemployment rose. In the face of this economic stagnation, members of both parties recognized that we needed an investment recovery to generate greater job creation. That's why they were open to the president's tax reforms.

As the chairman of the President's Council of Economic Advisers, I saw the tax reform negotiations firsthand. I watched a proposal that ordinarily would have been a purely Republican priority become an opportunity for collaboration. To win bipartisan support, President Bush included elements in the tax plan that appealed to Democrats. Likewise, Congressional Democrats were willing to consider the president's plan because they saw that it would help move the country toward a long-term goal: higher investment and higher employment.

Contrast that sense of shared purpose to today's world, where some politicians say, "Let's just raise taxes," or "Let's just cut these programs." Politicians make these kinds of big policy proposals all the time, but they rarely answer the most obvious and important question of all: toward what end?

There's a reason the most successful CEOs articulate where

---

30 www.pbs.org/newshour/bb/white_house/jan-june01/bush_
speech.html

they want to take a company before they say how they'll get there. If everyone involved agrees on a goal, then they have a way to measure their success. When presented with two paths, people can clearly compare one idea to another. But without a destination at the end of those paths, each person is free to retreat to absolutist positions – and there's no way to truly measure which will lead to greater success.

Solving our nation's challenges isn't a technical problem, as many in the media seem to believe. They think we need an expert to come in and do X or Y. But in most cases, the problem isn't technical – it's political. We don't have leaders who are forced to articulate their objectives and describe how they'd get there.

That's what needs to change. We need our leaders to stop moving from fight to fight – and to start telling us where they want to go. We need leaders who will be honest about the tradeoffs involved and the obstacles ahead. And we need leaders with vision, who can map out a better future for our country – and then take the steps we need to get there together.

NO LABELS VOICES
ALICE RIVLIN
FORMER OMB DIRECTOR AND VICE CHAIR
OF THE FEDERAL RESERVE

Today in Washington, D.C. most people think of the words "bipartisan solution" the way they think of the tooth fairy. It's a nice idea – until you grow up and realize it's a fantasy. But I've seen that fantasy become a reality many times, including twice in the last few years.

Since 2010, I've served on two major bipartisan commissions on the budget, one of which I co-chaired. The first was the Domenici-Rivlin Debt Reduction Task Force, and the second was the Simpson-Bowles Commission. In both cases, the members of these commissions started by agreeing on a common goal: reducing the size of the U.S. debt to below

60 percent of GDP. Once we'd agreed on that objective, it gave us a framework for discussing how to get there.

In the Domenici-Rivlin task force, we had another stipulation as well. We didn't just agree that we wanted to reduce the rate of debt growth. We also agreed that we wouldn't immediately rule out *any* means of getting there.

These two conditions enabled the task force members to work through the problem systematically – looking at all the options. First, we focused on slowing the growth of entitlements. Then we looked at slowing the growth of discretionary spending. But even once we'd agreed on some quite drastic recommendations on those points, the whole group – Republicans and Democrats alike – realized that we couldn't get there without some revenue increases as well.

At that point, we turned to tax reform. And once we looked at our options, we realized we could actually devise a simpler, more progressive tax structure. It would raise more revenue with lower rates, while being friendlier to economic growth. So we added this tax reform piece to the final plan we proposed.

If we had proposed this idea at the beginning, it almost certainly would have been viewed as a nonstarter. But we were ultimately able to agree on this major decision in the end largely because we had established a shared objective up front.

Domenici-Rivlin achieved unanimity, while Simpson Bowles only achieved a majority. But both of these commissions demonstrated that a group of people from different political parties could reach major agreement on contentious issues. Today, both parties need to learn the same lesson. In fact, our Constitution gives them no other choice. Our government is set up to force collaboration and dialogue. Even if all the branches of government were controlled by one party, we would *still* need the House, the Senate, and the Executive branch to find ways to work together.

Short of amending the Constitution to create a parliamentary system – which is not going to happen – we must break the gridlock by restoring dialogue and cooperation right now. That's the only way we can solve public problems and achieve big goals. It's going to take leadership from Congress and the White House – and we need that leadership now more than ever.

NO LABELS VOICES
DAVE WALKER
FORMER UNITED STATES COMPTROLLER GENERAL;
FOUNDER AND CEO OF THE COMEBACK AMERICA INITIATIVE

Management 101 says that if you want to maximize success, mitigate risk and ensure sustainability for a better future, you need to have three things: a plan, a budget and a set of desired outcomes or goals. The United States has been a republic since 1789 and we have none of those. We're zero for three. That's a strikeout. It's no wonder we have so many problems and ongoing political controversies.

It's important to rally the nation around a set of principles and values that can bring people together rather than divide them. And it's equally important to determine a set of common goals for the greater good. By working together across party lines and bridging ideological divides, it's possible to agree on a set of principles, values and goals that can break the gridlock in Washington and help pave the way for a better future. This has to happen – and I have demonstrated that it can.

In 2012, I traveled around the country to 27 states. I conducted various town hall meetings, and went to many college campuses and gatherings of business and community leaders to talk about the country's fiscal challenges. After discussing the gravity of our financial situation to a gathering of voters in two special town hall meetings, 97 percent of the group agreed that putting our finances in order should be a top priority for the president and the Congress. Then we got around 92 percent agreement on a set of principles and values to accomplish that objective.

Next, we offered a range of paths forward to achieve that goal, such as tax, Social Security, Medicare and Medicaid, health care, defense, management and political reforms. We got anywhere from 77 to 90 percent agreement on the proposed reforms. You can't get much better than that.

When I became U.S. Comptroller General in 1998 and head of the GAO (then called the General Accounting Office), the agency, in existence since 1921, had never had a strategic plan. In order to "lead by example," we began to develop one, and in January 2000 rolled it out. It's the closest thing the U.S. government has to a comprehensive and government-wide strategic plan. We used that plan to reorganize and reform the agency (including changing the agency's name to the Government Accountability Office). Eight years later, we had a 13 percent smaller staff, were 50 percent more productive, had three times the outcome-based results and were generating a $110 return on every dollar invested in the agency.

It's pretty basic. If you don't have a plan, you're flying blind. Right now, the federal government is flying blind in a mountain of debt with huge unfunded obligations that threaten our future position in the world, our future standard of living, our future national security and even our future domestic tranquility. And our fiscal challenge is only one of many challenges we face.

Washington is badly broken. We have a high degree of hyperpartisanship and a great ideological divide. It's important that we take steps to look longer and broader and to focus on common goals and desired outcomes in order to bring people together rather than divide them apart. Once both sides agree on a set of shared objectives, Congress should use these goals to inform new legislation and to guide its reauthorization, appropriations and oversight responsibilities. It's critically important that we have a strategic plan if we're ever going to break the gridlock. The time to act is now!

FROM SINGAPORE TO INDIA TO CHINA: STRATEGY IN ACTION

BY GOVERNOR JON HUNTSMAN
NO LABELS HONORARY CO-CHAIR

During my career, I've lived overseas four times and traveled to countless foreign countries. From Singapore to Brazil to the United Kingdom, they've been very different places. But most of them have had one very important thing in common: They've had national strategies. As countries, they've had clear ideas about where they need to go, and how they want to get there. Today, they are taking clear steps to strengthen their economies and their nations as a whole.

Right now, the United States is competing with these nations. But instead of pursuing clear goals to strengthen our future, our government stumbles along. We've fallen behind domestically, and we've tarnished our image internationally. We're moving from political crisis to political showdown, with no end in sight, and no plans for our future prosperity.

It doesn't have to be this way. When I ran for governor of Utah, my first shot at public office, I did what any sensible American would do: I drew up a plan. A plan that was short on politics and long on solutions.

Right away, I brought together experts and stakeholders from across our state. Citizens, small business leaders, academics, and a whole lot of other people offered ideas. In the end, we put together a ten-point plan for Utah, and I made clear that if I were elected, that was the strategy I was going to pursue.

The idea behind that ten-point plan was simple: we needed to make our economy stronger and more competitive. We saw that there were practical steps that could get us to those goals – not because one party said so, but because they were the right ideas for our state.

I was lucky enough to win that election. So once I got to the governor's office, the work began. I started consulting with members of both parties, making the case for why this plan was right for our state. I told them why I thought it would help us get ahead. And eventually, enough Democrats and Republicans got behind this shared agenda for our state. By the time I left office, we had implemented every single one of our ten original goals.

You might think that the only way to reach any kind of bipartisan agreement was to settle on watered-down, small-bore proposals. But the truth is, many of these were ambitious undertakings. We fundamentally reformed Utah's tax code to essentially implement a flat tax. We improved primary education and the colleges in our state. We worked to build our state's infrastructure so that it lived up to the promise of the 21st century.

By the time we were done, the results were clear. We had the lowest unemployment and the highest rates of economic growth in the nation. Our state's economy was growing the fastest in the nation. According to the Pew Foundation, we were also the best managed state in the nation. Everybody in Utah felt uplifted by this bipartisan success.

This was one of those increasingly rare instances in politics where we were able to put the will of the people at the forefront of politics. And it was only possible because we brought both parties together around a shared vision reflecting the collective interests of the state.

We did it in Utah – and we can do it as a country. Today our leaders need to stop focusing on narrow interests and start putting the will of the American people before politics.

The American people don't want political dysfunction. They want us to solve the biggest problems facing our country today. That's why I firmly believe that we need a national strategy for economic competitiveness – something that will keep us focused on the next generation and not the next election cycle. Something that allows us to put country first, well before the interests of political parties. I'm delighted that this book offers the first steps toward that goal.

WHY I JOINED:
THE BEST WAY FORWARD
FOR OUR COUNTRY

BY SENATOR JOE LIEBERMAN
NO LABELS HONORARY CO-CHAIR

During my 24 years in the U.S. Senate, I never introduced a significant legislative proposal unless I could find at least one Republican colleague who was willing to cosponsor it. I didn't adopt this policy so much as a matter of moral principle, although I did think it was the right thing to do. I did it mostly as a matter of practicality. I knew that without bipartisan support, there was no chance that my legislative proposal would pass and become a law. It was clear to me that if I wanted to get something done for my constituents and my country, I had to work across party lines.

There was one other thing I knew I had to do to be a productive legislator: I had to be willing to compromise. I don't mean compromise principles. I mean understanding that, in a legislative body as diverse as the U.S. Congress, whose members represent almost 320 million Americans, there would naturally be a broad spectrum of opinion. If I would only support legislation that included 100 percent of what I wanted, I would probably end up with zero percent – nothing – and so would Congress and our constituents.

While partisan, ideological, and special interest pressures work against it, compromise is the only way Congress and the president have ever achieved anything big for our country. In the piece he has written for this book, Jim Baker, who was President Reagan's Chief of Staff, writes: "I can remember the president repeatedly telling me that he'd rather get 80 percent of what he wanted than go over the cliff with his flag flying."

Interestingly, Sen. Ted Kennedy had a similar agreement with the various conservative Republicans who were his ranking members when he chaired Senate committees. If they agreed on 80 percent or even 60 percent of the issues on a big legislative proposal, they would put aside the areas of disagreement and move forward together to enact what they agreed upon.

As I look back at my time in the Senate, the accomplishments I feel best about all involved bipartisan cooperation and compromise: working with Sens. George Mitchell and John Chafee on the Clean Air Act Amendments of 1990; with Sens. Bob Dole, Joe Biden, and John McCain during the '90s to convince our government to act to stop the post-Cold War aggression and genocide in the Balkans; with Rep. Jack Kemp on urban enterprise zones; with Sens. Susan Collins and Fred Thompson to create the Department of Homeland Security and reform our intelligence agencies after the terrorist attacks of 9-11; and again with Sen. Collins to repeal the discriminatory "Don't Ask, Don't Tell" policy of the U.S. military.

As time went on, these kinds of accomplishments became harder and harder to achieve even though such initiatives are why members of Congress work so hard to get elected in the first place.

Why did this happen? Why have Congress and the president stopped working across party lines and compromising to get things done and solve problems? There are a number of reasons, including districts gerrymandered along partisan lines, candidates' dependency on big money from partisan, ideological, or special interest groups, and an increasingly partisan and ideological media.

The result is a government that leaves problems unsolved until they become crises and a political process that drains the natural optimism from the American people.

I joined No Labels because I believe it offers more hope

of curing what ails America's government than any other movement that exists today, and because more and more elected officials are recognizing the truth of the old wisdom that good government is good politics.

Consider this list of strengths. No Labels:

- Is not a centrist or moderate organization. It is an all-inclusive political movement that welcomes everyone, from left to right across the political spectrum, willing to work together to achieve big goals for our country.
- Has a proven track record of ideas and action, including legislation that has been signed into law.
- Has a growing constituency – a grassroots national movement of over 500,000 citizens, including 110 college chapters, and nearly 60 members of Congress from both parties who have joined an official bipartisan caucus of Problem Solvers – and has won support from an impressive group of leaders in the private sector.
- Is respected enough on Capitol Hill to have earned a recent Senate hearing on the subject of "Government Through Goal Setting."

I believe No Labels is the best response to today's widespread yearning among the American people for our government to start working for us again.

The big idea that has attracted so much support is the simple notion that if we look beyond partisan labels we can focus on the goals that most of us share for our country. Once we agree to these goals, we can sit down together, discuss how to achieve them, and lay out a plan – a National Strategic Agenda. That is the simple concept described in the pages of this book.

I hope that after you read about our vision you will decide to join us. Together, we can ensure that America's future will be, not just as good as our past, but even better.

THE ART OF THE POSSIBLE

BY GOVERNOR JOHN ENGLER
NO LABELS ADVISORY BOARD MEMBER

I often think of the passage of welfare reform in the mid-1990s as a prime example of government working as it is supposed to – with opposing sides coming together around big and important goals and then moving ahead to make real progress.

If you look back at that legislation, you can see a thousand reasons why it might not have succeeded. After the 1994 election, the gulf between the two parties often seemed unbridgeable. President Clinton and House Speaker Newt Gingrich crossed swords – and sharp words – on many of the urgent issues of the day. House Republicans' Contract with America, a list of their top priorities, had virtually no support from Democrats. Even House and Senate Republicans were often at odds.

But when you look at the passage of welfare reform, one of the tenets of the Contract with America, you can also see clearly why it *did* succeed, becoming a law that has been called the most significant social legislation of the last quarter of the 20th century. The key to passage was a goal that both Democrats and Republicans – in Congress and among many of the nation's governors – enthusiastically believed in and worked toward.

For all the different points of view, everyone agreed that the welfare system was badly broken. And everyone wanted to shift from an oppressive system to one that reinforced the value of work. That became the shared objective, the starting point for wide-ranging discussions and negotiations. Ultimately, we ended up with a system that included financial support but also incentives to help people move back to the workforce.

There were many points of departure regarding the kinds of incentives, how to monitor the program, how to support families who remained trapped even with additional services and support. Further, President Clinton twice vetoed versions of the bill that contained Medicaid block grants to the states that many Republicans were seeking but which were strongly opposed by many Democrats. Yet for all the sticking points, vast agreement on the big goal – turning welfare into a system based on work – led to legislation that allowed both parties to claim victory and support the sweeping reforms.

Governors learn quickly that they have to lead this way. They're held accountable for running a government, balancing a budget, delivering services. They cannot accept gridlock and deadlock as a mode of operating. Neither should our elected leaders at the national level.

As governor of Michigan, I was very much a believer in the philosophy that politics is the art of the possible. Sure, we can divide into warring camps, issue news releases, and get nothing done. Or we can sit down with each other, recognize and accept that we have different points of view and look for ways to solve problems and make progress together.

Believe me, I know it's easier said than done. Sometimes the differences seem so immense that it takes creative, outside-the-box thinking, and serious effort. I've seen my share of stalemates. For many years, for instance, intense debate over public school funding raged and dominated Michigan politics. It seemed like every legislative session was spent on the issue. Finally, in 1993, I signed legislation eliminating the use of property taxes that had been the means of funding public schools since Michigan became a state. Unfortunately, that practice had resulted in rich school districts and poor districts. I was seeking reforms that would improve the education system across the board – a goal everyone supported – but there was little agreement within the legislature about how to proceed. How we funded the schools was key to both achieving equity and fundamental educational reforms.

Democrats wanted to increase income taxes to finance schools. Republicans argued that an increase in the state sales tax was preferable. When we realized there would never be a meeting of the minds on the financing issue, we came up with a novel solution that satisfied both parties but required good faith among all.

First, the Democrats and Republicans each wrote their plans as they envisioned them. The Democratic plan – increasing the income tax – required a vote of the Legislature to pass. The Republican plan – increasing the sales tax – could be accomplished only by a Constitutional amendment voted on by the people.

So here's what we did: Republicans agreed to lend their support to the Democratic plan – even though they didn't favor it – so it would pass in the Legislature and become law. Then, the Democrats agreed to put the Republican plan on the ballot – even though they didn't favor that plan – so the citizens of the state would have a chance to vote it up or down. That way, we all realized, if the people of the state voted against the increase in sales taxes, the Democratic plan of higher income taxes would be enacted by the Legislature and would be the law. If citizens voted for the sales tax increase, then our Republican plan would replace the Democratic plan and become law.

As you might imagine, this idea required a great deal of trust on both sides. We had established that trust. In March 1994, the amendment raising the sales tax was put on the ballot, passed overwhelmingly, and to this day remains the basis for funding education in Michigan. We couldn't have solved the problem without good faith among our elected officials, the political leadership to tackle the issue in a bipartisan fashion, and a goal that everyone believed important.

There are plenty of opportunities for that sort of bipartisan problem solving today. We all want a government that works, a Defense Department that keeps the nation safe, water that is clean, roads that are in good shape, jobs for ourselves and our children, and a country that stands for freedom.

The four goals of the No Labels National Strategic Agenda

are the perfect starting point since we know they are priorities for most Americans. Other areas of overwhelming agreement exist, as well. Almost everyone thinks we ought to fund a highway bill for multiple years. I think most people agree we need some sort of common-sense immigration policy. Measures to enhance cyber security enjoy bipartisan support.

Many of our presidents who worked well with Congress did so because, with evenly split legislative bodies, they had to. They adopted the philosophy, often cited by Ronald Reagan, that an 80 percent friend is not a 20 percent enemy.

It's imperative that the next president of the United States embrace this approach. The problems facing our nation today are too urgent to be tied up by rigid partisanship. In the election cycle, we need more than political candidates simply assuring us they will work with their adversaries. Promises, we know, don't always translate to progress. We have to ask the candidates how they plan to tackle problems, how they plan to develop working relationships with the opposition, and how they plan to break the cycle of gridlock.

That's where No Labels plays a unique and critical role. As we head into the presidential primary season, the No Labels National Strategic Agenda with its goals for the nation and specific steps for constructive bipartisan action is exactly what the presidential candidates ought to be asked about. It's exactly what ought to be discussed in the debates. And it's exactly the approach that the next person who takes the oath of office should adopt to be an effective leader and to keep America prosperous and strong.

FROM GOALS TO RESULTS: LESSONS FROM TWO DECADES IN THE SENATE

BY SENATOR KAY BAILEY HUTCHISON
NO LABELS ADVISORY BOARD MEMBER

Early in my 20-year Senate career, I began an effort to make same-sex education available in public schools. From the start, the idea was met with fierce opposition from a few education groups and those who worried that if schools, or even classes, for girls and boys were separate, they might not be equal. Year after year, the idea of same-sex education in public schools was knocked down.

It wasn't until we honed in on a goal that we all had in common – proponents and opponents of same-sex education alike – that we found a pathway to success.

Those of us who studied and cared deeply about this issue realized that, whatever our position on the subject was, we had one thing in common: We all agreed that education should fit the individual student's needs as much as possible. *That* then became our goal. That translated to giving school districts and even individual school principals options so they could tailor programs to the best interests of their particular student bodies. Those options included offering same-sex schools or classes if principals and school districts felt such an approach would be most beneficial to students.

After very clearly defining the goal – the first essential element – we moved on to the next key step: assembling a bipartisan coalition. Fortunately, a number of women senators in both parties, including some who'd appreciated the all-girls educations they'd had, supported the effort. With co-sponsors like then-Sen. Hillary Clinton of New York and Sen. Barbara Mikulski of Maryland from the Democratic side and Sen. Susan Collins of Maine and myself from the Republican side, we proposed an amendment to the education bill in June 2001 that would make single-sex education legal in public school and eligible for federal funding. It passed by unanimous consent in the Senate and was eventually signed into law by President Bush.

Both sides had pretty clear-cut differences, but also a very clear-cut goal. And that goal ultimately brought together Republicans and Democrats – and brought about success.

My partnerships with Democrats were invaluable to my years in the Senate – and the key to everything I'm proud to have accomplished.

Another one of my priorities upon entering the Senate had been changing the laws regarding individual retirement accounts so that stay-at-home spouses could invest in IRA's and build financial security for their later years. I found an enthusiastic co-sponsor in Sen. Mikulski, who worked hard to marshal her Democratic troops. Together, we won passage of this important legislation, which has ensured that spouses who stay at home to take care of family responsibilities – generally women, although the last decade has brought increasing numbers of men – are no longer at a disadvantage when it comes to retirement security.

Sen. Clinton sought my help in building Republican support for legislation that would allow widows of veterans who receive survivor benefits to keep those benefits if she remarries after age 57. Before that, surviving spouses who remarried were not allowed to receive these benefits.

The list goes on: Then-Sen. John Kerry and I worked for years on a plan for an infrastructure bank, a public-private partnership that provided a blueprint for what is now being shepherded through Congress by Sen. Kirsten Gillibrand of New York. California Sen. Dianne Feinstein and I worked together on a bill that resulted in millions of dollars for breast cancer research through postage stamp fees.

In all of these cases, and many more, my Democratic partners and I didn't care about who got the credit. We didn't care about scoring political points for our party. We cared about doing what we were elected to do, which was enact legislation that would improve life for our constituents and all Americans.

Sadly, this sense of collegiality and shared mission has deteriorated badly since I left public office in 2013. Many in Congress today embrace a rigid, my-way-or-the-highway agenda, and are all too willing to let the rancor and rough-and-tumble of campaign season persist even after they've moved into their Capitol Hill offices.

I am optimistic because I still see flashes of people working in a bipartisan spirit and without regard to partisan politics. Even on an issue as weighty and complicated as the Iran nuclear deal, for instance, members of Congress in both parties appeared to take their votes seriously and leave partisan calculations out of their decision-making.

These instances of good-faith problem solving need to be more than just occasional flashes. They need to become as much a part of the culture in Washington as the statues and marble corridors. It will take a willingness on the part of members of Congress to look for common ground with political opponents and sit down with those colleagues to hammer out solutions. It will also take a president who is willing to engage with Congress and be a part of the process, preferably at the beginning stages of the legislative process rather than the end.

No Labels has come up with a way to make this happen, which is why I'm pleased to be a part of this movement. They have identified four big-picture goals that I believe are imperative to keeping America strong. These are simple, clear goals on which we all should be able to agree. The organization is also putting its agenda squarely before the 2016 presidential candidates so voters will be able to see very plainly which candidates are ready to embrace a problem-solving approach; one that involves accountability and action – not just lip service.

If we can accomplish the four No Labels goals, and bring

both Republicans and Democrats on board to work together with a problem-solving president, we can all feel more confident that America will remain the greatest nation on Earth.

IT SHOULDN'T TAKE A CRISIS

BY SENATOR EVAN BAYH
NO LABELS ADVISORY BOARD MEMBER

If we lived in times of peace and robust prosperity, a political system marked by partisan gridlock might be acceptable. Unfortunately, we don't live in such times. The nation faces significant challenges both on the economic and national security front. Left unaddressed, these problems will only fester and grow, eventually endangering the future of the country for all of us and our children.

The issues facing us today require productive debate that will lead to national consensus. They require action. They require a governing class that rises above partisan politics to put the welfare of the country and its citizens first.

During my 12 years in the Senate, our political leaders met this challenge several times, but generally during moments of crisis. The first occurred one week into my Senate career when, after the House had impeached President Clinton, we began the process of a Senate trial. Since it was the first such constitutional crisis since 1868, there were no rules for how to conduct this sort of proceeding.

My colleagues and I gathered in the old Senate chamber to try to figure it out. Not surprisingly, in the midst of such a politically heated atmosphere, our talks were partisan and acrimonious – and were going nowhere. Finally, we designated a representative for each party – Sen. Ted Kennedy of Massachusetts for the Democrats, Sen. Phil Gramm of Texas for the Republicans, one as liberal, the other as conservative as you can get – to work out an agreement. Within a day, they hashed out a fair and well-considered compromise, which the Senate passed unanimously.

As politically volatile as these times were, we all knew that if we made a mockery of trying to remove the president of the United States, the country would be deeply damaged. So even with hardened partisan positions on both sides, we were able to work together for the welfare of the country, rise above political considerations, and do the right thing. The trial went on, of course, and was conducted objectively. The president was acquitted. The country was able to get on with its business.

We saw an even more remarkable display of unity after the 9/11 attacks. A few days after that horrific event, senators who were in Washington or able to get back to Capitol Hill gathered in the Senate dining room. It was one of the rare times – perhaps the *only* time I can recall – when there was no feeling of being a Democrat or a Republican. Everyone was thinking like an American. Our only consideration was coming together to figure out how best to protect the country.

In a third instance, at the peak of the financial crisis with the country on the cusp of a complete meltdown in 2008, members of Congress had to decide whether to vote for a financial package that would save the big banks but was deeply unpopular with our constituents. My calls and letters were running 10,000 to 1 against the package (the Troubled Asset Relief Program, or TARP). I completely understood why. Citizens wondered why the U.S. Treasury would rush in to help out the large companies and financial institutions that were failing, but not the average worker or homeowner who was struggling. If there had been a way to help the latter but not the former, we would have. But sadly, there was not. The reality was, as bad as these times were, if we let these large institutions fail, we'd be plunging the country into greater depths of the recession, with tens of millions more bankruptcies and jobs lost. Average people on Main Street would have been ruined, too.

Most of us decided that, though voting for the package was distasteful and potentially damaging to us politically, it was necessary. The bill passed in the Senate 75-25 on a bipartisan basis.

House members came to the same conclusion, although not immediately. The House first voted the bill down, and then saw the stock market drop 700 points in an hour. Lawmakers came back the next day and passed the bill, which President George W. Bush then signed into law.

Again, Democrats and Republicans came together, realizing that failure to do so could have put the country in great peril.

It shouldn't take a constitutional crisis or a terrorist attack or a financial calamity to propel our political leaders to work together. It shouldn't be the rare exception to the rule. But that's where we are. It's why movements like No Labels are so desperately needed.

The No Labels concept of a National Strategic Agenda built around big, specific goals is a powerful idea because it provides a toolkit for this kind of across-the-aisle problem solving with a timeline and metrics for success and accountability. This is no experiment. We know this process works. I've even had a rare opportunity to see what happens when the two political parties are *required* to work together.

When I was elected governor of Indiana in 1988, the state House of Representatives was split 50/50 by party and thus deadlocked on everything, even the selection of committee chairs and a Speaker of the House. With no resolution in sight, the legislature decided to choose two Speakers and two chairs of every committee – one from each party – who would alternate days that they'd preside.

It was an unorthodox solution, and one nearly everyone thought could be a recipe for chaos. But, in fact, it worked so well and the legislators were so productive that there's now a plaque on the wall of the Indiana House of Representatives commemorating the historic divided House of 1989-'90. More compromises were struck, more legislation was passed, more respect and relationships were fostered because the Democrats and Republicans *had* to work together.

Again, it shouldn't take a crisis or, in this case, an accident of electoral politics, to force our elected officials to work together.

This has to become more than an aberration, and the public must insist on it!

We're already seeing the public's immense frustration with politics as usual in presidential polls showing that the majority of Republican voters prefer candidates with no government experience whatsoever. They're reflecting a real disdain for the way government is being operated by those in positions of power.

The public gets it. The governing class not so much. But the strongest instinct for most politicians is self-preservation. My hunch is, if it becomes clear they will get the boot if they don't start solving problems and producing results, our political leaders will start behaving responsibly.

That's what No Labels is all about. It's about encouraging citizens to tell our leaders, Enough already! We've got serious problems we need to address, and we want our elected officials to tackle them in a responsible and productive way. Sure, there will be disagreements and areas to argue about and debate. Yes, our politics is more divided today than in decades past. But in the end, some progress is better than none. In the end, we have to make a course correction for the sake of our country and our future.

NO LABELS VOICES
STEPHEN HEINTZ
PRESIDENT, ROCKEFELLER BROTHERS FUND

It was during an "involuntary sabbatical" in 2012 that I decided to focus my attention on the current state of our democracy.

In the early phase of my career, I'd spent 15 years in politics and government in Connecticut and had become a bit jaded. Even in the 1970s and '80s, it was already apparent that money was far too prevalent and influential, and that politics was more of a competitive sport than an effort to get things done. After the Berlin Wall fell, I moved to Eastern Europe and worked to help strengthen the transitions to democracy across the region.

Being there for the first decade after the collapse of communism was very exciting and inspiring, and when I returned to America, I was ready to work to revitalize our own democracy.

When I joined the Rockefeller Brothers Fund in 2001, we created a grant-making program to do just that – try to help strengthen and revitalize American democracy. Then in 2012, I had one of those moments that really wakes you up when I was diagnosed with a rare form of leukemia. I spent a year getting chemotherapy and then had a successful bone marrow transplant. Between hospitalization and my time recuperating at home, I was out of work for about nine months.

After I was diagnosed, I made the decision to try to be very disciplined and use the time to study and think about the state of our democracy. I read current literature, historical literature, books, journals, and articles, many of which described the decline in our political culture, the tearing at our social fabric, the growth of economic inequality and decline in economic opportunity.

It was striking to me that a lot of the literature pointed to the same 30-year period starting in the late 1970s when we went off track, in part because of globalization, advances in technology and radical changes in the economy, but also, in part, by design – by political decisions and changes in public policy. The more I read, the angrier I got. I concluded that we are adrift as a country and we don't share a sense of national purpose.

We have had this common purpose at moments of great crisis in our history including the country's founding. The Declaration of Independence is an elegant statement of national purpose. There have been other such moments: the Civil War, the fight against fascism, the Cold War, the mission to put a man on the moon, our coming to terms and coming together around civil rights and gender rights. These were moments where the nation struggled, but ultimately came together and found a sense of shared national purpose.

We have to come together and once again be the America of our collective dream. It's going to require a strategic agenda for the country, based on big national goals that we need to accomplish in this century. And then it's going to take a plan for reforming the political process so we can accomplish those goals, so we can have a truly functioning democratic system.

One of the books I read during my "sabbatical" was a volume commissioned by Nelson Rockefeller in the mid-1950s, when he was chairman of the board here at the RBF, and aspired to be president of the United States. He realized he needed a platform of ideas and a brain trust to help him develop the substantive ideas for a presidential campaign. He brought together leaders from business, academia, philanthropy, the nonprofit sector, the faith community, and trade unions, and hired staff that included a young Henry Kissinger from Harvard. They spent four years working in sub-panels – on topics ranging from arts and culture to national security – and issued a series of papers with national goals and very specific proposals for each topic that became a book, "Prospects for America," published in 1961.

Although Nelson obviously didn't get to be president of the United States, John F. Kennedy and later Lyndon B. Johnson used some of the material, and a number of the ideas became national policy.

We have to engage in a similar process of analysis and goal setting today, one that's not just limited to a blue-ribbon commission, but that includes the grassroots engagement of hundreds of thousands if not millions of Americans. It will take a major national conversation over the next couple years – a very serious dialogue about the kinds of goals we want to achieve, the kind of country we want to be, and the kinds of reforms that are necessary to accomplish those purposes.

LEARNING FROM BUSINESS: A RECIPE FOR NATIONAL SUCCESS

BY RON SHAICH
FOUNDER AND CEO, PANERA BREAD

For a businessman like Ron Shaich, strategic thinking comes naturally. That's why he's been able to found two of the most successful restaurant concepts in America: Au Bon Pain and Panera Bread. No matter what, Ron has always had a clear sense of where his business needs to go. That's why he's been so successful. And he strongly believes that the United States needs to catch up with this kind of thinking.

— Jon

As a CEO, my most important imperative is figuring out what actions we have to take today to get us to where we want to be tomorrow. In every meeting, regardless of topic, the most important questions have always been the same. What are we trying to achieve? What are our criteria for success? And what do we need to do to make sure we accomplish our goals?

This was what we discussed in our very first conversations relative to starting Panera Bread. At the time, the restaurant world was essentially split between fine dining and fast food. And within the world of fast food, most operators sought to deliver mass-produced, lower-quality fare at very low prices.

We looked at that and realized a significant number of people wanted something better. They wanted food they could respect served by people with self respect. They wanted it served in an environment that engaged them. They were willing to pay a bit more, but they also wanted something different – something more – coming back across the counter.

From that moment onwards, our strategy was clear. We decided to fill in that niche and offer that something more. Once we'd made that overarching decision, every other action we took – from developing the items on our menu to creating the layout of our restaurants – was designed to bring that goal into reality. It was all about building a differentiated alternative for the guest. And in the decades since, we've stayed true to that central, guiding plan.

There were times when we were tested, but we never wavered from that fundamental strategy. When the recession hit, many restaurants started cutting back on costs. We were under a great deal of pressure to do that, too. But we knew cutting costs would mean longer lines, dirtier restaurants, and lower-quality food. In short, it would go against our fundamental strategy of delivering something more.

So at the height of the recession, instead of pulling back, we decided to invest, consistent with our strategy. Indeed, we chose to improve the quality of the experience because we still believed that was what mattered. As a result we started rolling out new, innovative menu items and invested in extra labor in our cafes. We also chose to increase our growth rate by 50 percent to take advantage of the opportunities for high quality investment that the recession provided.

In the end, we saw our profits skyrocket during the depths of the recession and our stock followed course, roughly doubling in size during the same period (January 2008 to mid 2009), which set the stage for even more impressive growth in the years that followed. And that was possible only because we looked beyond the short-term pressures of the moment, and kept our eyes trained on the plan that really mattered.

When I look at Congress right now, I see them making the exact opposite choice. Our leaders aren't thinking about how we're going to compete in the long term. They're almost entirely focused on getting through the next election or the next legislative session. But if one focuses only on the immediate future, I can promise an outcome similar to that shared by many of my competitors – the ones who optimized their short-term profitability and provided Panera the opportunity to leap ahead of them.

Ultimately, I would argue that if you're a leader, you have a responsibility not only to survive, but to lead. And if you are an elected official you have a responsibility to leave this country better than you found it. That's why I believe our leaders in Washington need to look beyond the issue of the week. They need to stop focusing on keeping score and political games. Instead, they need to finally agree on a shared strategy for our country. Ultimately, that's how we'll regain our competitive advantage as a nation and that's how we will continue to succeed.

NO LABELS VOICES
KATHERINE M. GEHL
PRESIDENT AND CEO, GEHL FOODS, INC.

In business, we would have tremendous problems if we didn't have a strategy everyone understood and was invested in. We run a manufacturing company in the heartland, and like many manufacturing companies, we are going through a major transition from a traditional, command-and-control facility to the kind of world-class facility you need to be competitive in today's global economy.

That means more empowerment and opportunity for the employees, but also more accountability. It's a very different way of working for the 300 people at my company, and change is hard. There are trade-offs. People like doing things the way they're used to doing them. If the employees didn't have a shared understanding of our future vision, we would spend all our time on the negative aspects of the changes. Instead, a clearly communicated strategy can bring people aboard and enroll them in making the effort and taking action to reach the goal. A shared vision and strategy creates possibility both for the company and for employees as individuals.

I think the biggest promise for a national strategy lies in the opportunity it provides not only for enrolling leaders of both political parties, but even more importantly, for enrolling the citizens who have to support the direction and the difficult choices required – because change isn't easy.

It's essential to note, however, that we don't just have a strategy problem in this country. We have an execution problem. That's because the political parties, which are private organizations, exercise vast control over the process of both elections and governing. In addition to a strategic plan, we need to keep pressing for the reforms that No Labels has called for to help make Congress, the presidency and government work better and to get beyond partisan roadblocks.

It all ties together. If we don't change the way we do business, then our ability to execute our strategy and achieve our goals will be hampered. We need the initiatives that form the foundation of No Labels along with a National Strategic Agenda. That's a winning combination!

NO LABELS VOICES
ANDREW TISCH
CO-CHAIRMAN OF THE BOARD AND CHAIRMAN OF
THE EXECUTIVE COMMITTEE, LOEWS CORPORATION

Throughout my business career, I've found that the first step toward success is clarity of mission. If a mission is clear, it stands the greatest chance of being achieved and the greatest chance of rallying people together with unanimity of purpose.

That clarity of mission is what's missing in Washington today. There is no unanimity of vision. Instead, you've got two completely different groups that are battling for the hearts and minds of the public. Everyone is arguing about strategy, but there's no clarity on what the ultimate goal is. For our country to move forward, we need a very strong national agenda based on consensus and a clear set of goals.

I've seen the power of having a shared sense of mission. Several years ago, then-New York Mayor Mike Bloomberg proposed the idea of a contest among universities to build a new computer sciences and high-tech campus on Manhattan's Roosevelt Island. The whole concept seemed to be written so that Stanford University would win the contract. A lot of people at Cornell University, where I'm on the board of trustees, said, "Hey! This may be something that's good for Cornell as well as the community and plays to our core strengths." So without a tremendous amount of communication or coordination, a number of different groups at Cornell proceeded down the same path.

The mission was so strong in everyone's mind that there was absolutely no choreography necessary in order to get to where we had to be. Students, faculty, alumni, friends … everybody knew exactly what the mission was and was pulling in unison. One group was writing up the proposal. I used my political connections to make sure our voice was heard in city hall. Somebody else with strong connections to labor was off organizing labor groups and unions. Another group started an alumni petition. Everybody was working towards the same goal and ultimately Stanford was outflanked. We won in a head-to-head competition, and construction is well underway of this $2 billion campus.

When a company is in real trouble, you often see this kind of cohesive effort in turnaround management. A great CEO rallies the troops by letting everybody know exactly what the issues are and what success will look like and, importantly, how to get there. It's what we did when Loews took over Bulova in 1979. We turned around a small bankrupt watchmaker and made it a successful company by agreeing on what constituted success and then coming up with a plan to achieve that success. It took us five years to go from steep decline to the breakeven point, and then another couple of years to get to profitability.

Business tends to be more a dictatorship than a democracy. In the end, the CEO makes the decisions and faces the greatest consequences. But most great CEO's try to do things collaboratively. It's time our political leaders apply a bit of turnaround management, form a consensus and articulate a clear vision for this country. We have seen that happen after D-Day, in parts of the Kennedy and Reagan administrations and even after 9-11 for a while. And it's possible once again today – especially with the strong advocacy of a group like No Labels.

There's a quote I'm fond of that underscores the challenge we face today. The author is unknown, but the cautionary theme is worth pondering "A democracy is always temporary in nature; it simply cannot exist as a permanent form of government. A democracy will continue to exist up until the time that voters discover that they can vote themselves generous gifts from the public treasury. From the moment on, the majority always votes for the candidates who promise the most benefits from the public treasury, with the result that every democracy will finally collapse due to loose fiscal policy, which is always followed by a dictatorship.

> "The average age of the world's greatest civilizations from the beginning of history has been about 200 years. During those 200 years, these nations always progressed through the following sequence: From bondage to spiritual faith; from spiritual faith to great courage; from courage to liberty; from liberty to abundance; from abundance to selfishness; from selfishness to complacency; from complacency to apathy; from apathy to dependence; from dependence back to bondage."

We don't have to go this route. We can still come together to make our nation stronger. I think there's a critical mass at the center of our electorate – I call it the middle 80 percent – that will come together around a national agenda. And that's what it will take to move our country forward.

AMERICA'S LEADERSHIP CHECKLIST

BY MICHAEL USEEM
DIRECTOR, CENTER FOR LEADERSHIP AND
CHANGE MANAGEMENT, THE WHARTON SCHOOL

Michael Useem, a longtime scholar of leadership, has studied great leaders and leaders who have fallen short — and he has seen what it takes for a nation to succeed. As a professor at the University of Pennsylvania's Wharton business school, he continues to observe our country's elected leaders closely. In this chapter, he discusses the kind of leadership we need today — and the kind of leaders we should look for and vote for in elections to come — if we want to build consensus around a strong vision for our country.

— Joe

For the ideas in this volume to come to life, everybody's leadership will be vital. Otherwise, even the best ideas will never make it off the page.

Right now, however, many of our national leaders appear to be paralyzed, unable or unwilling to rise above the gridlock. They act as if they are hopelessly trapped by the political congestion we have all come to know too well.

It's understandable that many politicians might consider even the smallest, most commonsense initiatives to be futile in the face of Washington's gridlock. Why would any elected official pursue fresh thinking or big ideas when interest groups always seem ready to stand in the way and political landmines are always ready to explode?

In many ways this sense of resignation is understandable.

After all, the logjam on Capitol Hill is certainly among the worst of recent memory. For many in Washington, inaction seems the only feasible action.

But of course our history has been punctuated by moments far worse, and leaders during the hardest times have confronted far more intractable conflicts. Abraham Lincoln faced a break-away republic, Franklin Delano Roosevelt a world at war, and Nelson Mandela a ruthless regime. Yet each found a way forward where others saw none. They persisted, and they prevailed.

Our discords today are not as profound, and the stakes not as momentous, but our differences certainly do run very deep. And resolution of those differences – or our failure to resolve them – will undoubtedly define our country's direction for many years to come.

We know from experience that a nation's leadership has the greatest impact when a country is facing its greatest uncertainties, when the contentious issues are especially nettlesome, and when the most fateful decisions are particularly complex. It's thus times like these when a nation's leadership is most important – and when we need our leaders to reach for something greater than the pettiness of the moment.

In other words, we need *more* national leadership now, precisely because this is one of those very moments when exercising that leadership has become all the more impactful – and all the more difficult.

What will it take for our national leadership to break out of that deadlock? I've been studying leadership for quite some time, and I've found that the answer really requires no rocket science. In fact, the way forward for our leaders can be distilled to just a half-a-dozen plain old-fashioned leadership ingredients. This is what we will all want to see more of among those most responsible for the future of the country:

1. *Take charge:* Embrace action. If you are positioned to make a difference, no matter how modest, take responsibility.

2. *Define a vision and a strategy:* Formulate a clear and

powerful view of the solutions we want and a way of getting there.

3. *Communicate persuasively:* Characterize that vision and that strategy in ways people cannot forget.

4. *Embrace the front lines:* Stay close to those most directly engaged with the work of the initiative, drawing the best from each.

5. *Build leadership throughout the ranks:* Develop a capacity for all of us to help take charge, each in our own way.

6. *Place public interest first:* In communicating a vision, setting the strategy, and taking actions, common purpose always comes first, political self-interest last.

We have witnessed all of these qualities powerfully at work when Abraham Lincoln mobilized his "team of rivals" to save the Union, when Ronald Reagan and Tip O'Neill garnered budgets without brinksmanship, and even in everyday life when citizens get on with the business of getting things done.

These ideas might sound obvious, but they've been shockingly absent from our political discourse over the last several years. Instead of embracing the precepts to resolve real problems, too many of our elected officials have devolved into political gamesmanship. But if our leaders can embrace just a handful of very simple principles, we believe that a transformative moment lies ahead.

Gov. Jon Huntsman, Sen. Joe Lieberman and more than 70 members of Congress have already embraced these principles in building the problem-solving foundation that defines No Labels. And in doing so, they've already begun to change how Washington works.

Their active leadership – and our active leadership – has become essential for moving the No Labels ideas into reality. Together, our combined leadership can advance a genuine national strategy for a country that otherwise seems stuck in neutral or worse.

STRENGTH THROUGH COOPERATION: TWO VIEWS FROM THE OVAL OFFICE

BY MACK MCLARTY
WHITE HOUSE CHIEF OF STAFF
FOR PRESIDENT BILL CLINTON

One of my most enduring memories of my time as President Bill Clinton's White House Chief of Staff was sitting in the Roosevelt Room with Newt Gingrich and George Stephanopoulos. They weren't debating a policy dispute or hammering out a contentious bargain. They were counting votes, together.

It was November 17, 1993, and the House of Representatives was voting on the North American Free Trade Agreement (NAFTA) – an effort to create a vibrant North American market that reached from the Yukon to the Yucatan.

NAFTA had been negotiated by President George H.W. Bush's administration, but the Clinton administration was determined to see it through. President Clinton understood that in an age of globalization, America's future depended on competing with the rest of the world, not retreating from it.

This was an instance where the president and members of the opposing party not only agreed on a shared goal but actively worked together to secure it. Indeed, another enduring memory from that time was the Rose Garden event where President Carter, President Bush, and President Clinton stood shoulder to shoulder in calling for NAFTA's passage.

In the end, NAFTA passed both houses of Congress on a strongly bipartisan basis, but with more Republicans than

Democrats voting in favor. The President proudly signed the agreement into law. At the time, this was the most comprehensive free trade agreement on earth. In the years since, it's been vital to our nation's economic growth; today, U.S. trade with Canada and Mexico supports 14 million good U.S. jobs.

The Clinton years may be remembered for periods of partisan discord, but this was just one example of many where the two parties came together. The president and his staff savored any opportunity to work alongside the Republicans in Congress. We all liked it better when we could find common ground and work to achieve a common goal.

That was true with the 1996 Welfare-to-Work initiative that helped move millions of Americans from the welfare rolls to paid employment; the 1997 budget agreement that cut spending, cut the deficit, and set us on course for a balanced budget; and almost all major foreign policy issues. Both parties agreed on where we needed to go, and then we found a way to get there together.

If we had been able to agree on more shared goals, I'm sure the achievements would have been even more numerous. After all, we've also seen this approach work with incredible success at the state level. America's governors have legislatures to deal with, too. But they almost always find a way to work together, even if it means reaching across party lines.

As President Clinton wrote in *The New York Times* on the 10th anniversary of the welfare reform legislation, "This style of cooperative governing is anything but a sign of weakness. It is a measure of strength, deeply rooted in our Constitution and history, and essential to the better future that all Americans deserve, Republicans and Democrats alike."[31]

We need that same spirit in Washington today. We need the leaders of both parties in Washington to find a shared path forward once again. I believe that this is possible – and for the good of our country, I hope it happens soon.

---

31 www.nytimes.com/2006/08/22/opinion/22clinton.html; "How We Ended Welfare, Together," President Bill Clinton, *The New York Times*, August 22, 2006.

BY JAMES A. BAKER III
WHITE HOUSE CHIEF OF STAFF FOR PRESIDENT
RONALD REAGAN AND FORMER SECRETARY OF STATE

No one was more of an idealist than President Ronald Reagan. He believed in the noble concepts of American exceptionalism, and he possessed concrete notions about how to maintain it. Keep spending low, income taxes down, and get out of the way of the private sector so that it can be the world's most efficient economic engine.

But The Gipper was also a realist. He understood that Americans judge our presidents on more than their convictions and fanciful rhetoric. Americans also judge them by their accomplishments, by their ability to get things done in Washington – particularly when times get tough.

Few times were tougher than when Reagan was inaugurated in 1981. He faced an economy plagued by the so-called "misery index," with both inflation and unemployment hovering above 10 percent. *Newsweek* proclaimed that President Reagan had inherited "the most dangerous economic crisis since Franklin Roosevelt took office 48 years ago."

Reagan got to work, and he did what a leader should do. He built consensus around the objectives he wanted to achieve. He worked with the Democratic-controlled Congress toward the shared goal of economic revitalization – and almost immediately, he began to see success.

The President and the Democrats in Congress had real policy disagreements, of course. It wasn't always easy for them to work together. As Reagan's White House chief of staff at the time, I can remember the president and Democratic House Speaker Tip O'Neill yelling at one another during their negotiations in the Oval Office. They would go at it tooth-and-nail for long stretches. But once their business discussions had concluded, the two would retire for a drink and to tell Irish stories.

Eventually, they struck deals. Before the end of his first

year in office, Reagan and the Democratic-controlled Congress passed the Economic Recovery Tax Act of 1981, which, among other things, dropped the top tax rate from 70% to 50%. They later worked together to reduce the top rate to 28%.

Neither side got everything that it wanted in these negotiations. Taxes were lowered, as Reagan desired. But spending was not reduced, as he had hoped. Compromise was not a dirty word. It was a way to get things done.

Some in his party criticized President Reagan for not holding to his principles, for caving into Democrats. But I can remember the president repeatedly telling me that he'd rather get 80 percent of what he wanted than go over the cliff with his flag flying. With that approach incorporated into his DNA, Reagan ushered in an era of peace, prosperity and American conservatism.

The economy responded. By 1984, the "misery index" had been cut in half from its level when Reagan took office. Reagan's pro-growth policies resulted in 96 months of unbroken economic growth starting in 1983, the creation of 18 million new jobs during that same period, and the eradication of inflation and high interest rates.

Ronald Reagan knew how to fight when he had to. But he also knew when to work with the other side for the good of the country. He was a principled pragmatist. Our leaders in Washington should take a look at that Reagan playbook and take the same approach today.

CONCLUSION:
NOVEMBER 8, 2016

Think about what our country could look like with a set of shared goals and a national strategic agenda. Imagine how much better off we would be. Well, thanks to No Labels, we don't have to just imagine anymore. We can start building that stronger country today. The cause is urgent, and now is the time. Let's do this together.

— Jon and Joe

It's Tuesday, November 8, 2016. You've just woken up, gotten the kids off to school, and swung by the local community center to cast your vote before work. Today we're electing a new Congress and a new president of the United States.

It's time to ask: When you step out of the voting booth, what kind of country do you want to walk back into?

If we stay on the path we're on now, it's not hard to imagine what that country will look like. A hopelessly divided Washington. A president more devoted to party than to country. An opposition party more concerned with putting up obstacles than coming to the negotiating table. Elected leaders on all sides obsessed with scoring political points – and not many interested in the real challenges facing ordinary Americans.

In other words, it will be just like today. Except all of our problems will have gotten worse. Is that what you want to vote for?

Or do you want to choose a different path? A path that includes a problem-solving president and a functioning Congress. A path that includes a new governing process where we actually agree on where we need to go as a country – and then collaborate to find a way to get there together.

Imagine what this country could look like. Before the State of the Union, the president and the leader of the opposition meet to talk about their goals for the year. They offer an honest assessment of the progress we've made and where we still need to go. And when the president stands before the country to deliver his or her first State of the Union, both sides of the aisle stand up and applaud.

Imagine how much could be accomplished if, in the first 30 days of the next administration, the new president gathered the leaders of both parties together to decide on goals they would tackle together and commit to staying at the table until those goals were met.

Imagine what the halls of Congress could look like if members of different parties started meeting regularly to have frank and open discussions about where we need to go as a country. Suddenly, they aren't just trying to score political points or embarrass the other side. They're working to move our country forward. No one in Congress forgets about their deeply held beliefs or the areas where they disagree. But there are plenty of issues where they *can* agree – and when that happens, they don't just allow their different parties to drive them apart.

Instead of government shutdowns and crisis governance, we get a sensible budget every year that's designed to achieve a set of goals we've all agreed on. And before long, we'll be well on the way toward balancing that budget.

Instead of self-inflicted economic wounds, our leaders have come together and told the country that job creation is their top priority. And they didn't just talk about creating jobs – they started taking action. Now jobs are returning home, and all across the country men and women are returning to work and taking home paychecks that can support their families.

We're producing more and more energy at home, and we're using it in more sustainable ways. Within a few years, we won't need to import oil from unfriendly governments just to keep our country up and running. Instead, we've already seen a new energy economy start to blossom here at home. And it's a shift that comes with millions of good American jobs.

When you pass children on the street, you feel confident that our government will keep its sacred promises to our next generation. Social Security and Medicare are secure – and Americans who have worked all their lives are able to retire with the peace of mind and dignity they deserve.

As these challenges are addressed, our leaders are building momentum to take on even greater problems. For a long time, we've recognized that we need to do more to make sure every child in America has access to a world-class education. We've known that we need to do more to support research, development, and innovation here at home. It's been clear that we need to do better in so many ways – from improving health care to supporting small businesses to strengthening our national security.

All of these issues have plagued our country for years. We've all known it. But now that we've started fixing some of our most foundational problems, we finally have the resources – and the energy – to take the actions we need.

Most important of all, America has leaders who are actually leading once again. They've proven that they can actually still come together around important objectives. They've proven that they can still get things done. And it's clear that this is just the beginning.

This vision doesn't have to be a fantasy. Every one of these items should be common sense for our leaders in Washington. In fact, for a long time we would have thought this was the bare minimum a functioning government would get done. That's not too much to ask again. As a nation, we still have every element for success at our fingertips. America boasts the world's greatest universities, the greatest minds, an innovative potential just waiting to take off. We have men and women in every corner of this country aching to start new businesses and try out new ideas. And we have the rule of law that means they can do it.

Wherever you look in America, you see amazing potential. A manufacturing sector still poised for a renaissance. A natural gas boom that could power our future. The most amazing moment in technological history – with more great ideas percolating wherever you look.

Today our nation is more diverse, more resourceful, and more interconnected than ever before. We have so much working in our favor. We just need the leadership to take advantage of these strengths.

In the end, it all comes down to one last question: Are you happy with the way our government is working right now?

If you're content with how our government is operating, then this movement isn't for you. But if you're part of the vast majority of Americans who desperately want our leaders to start working together once again, then we need you. We need you to join our campaign to change politics in America. We need you to add your voice to our call for shared goals and a National Strategic Agenda.

Together, we need to call on every member of Congress and every candidate for office to get behind this campaign. Because above all, this campaign's success is going to take real leadership from Washington. We need leaders who will commit to work together, to find common goals, to work to achieve them without constant fighting and division.

We don't expect anyone to shed their identity when they join this movement. No one will ever have to check their principles or priorities at the door. And in fact, this diversity makes the movement stronger. It empowers our movement with the energy of every point on the political spectrum. It recognizes that great ideas can come from anywhere. This is a movement that will welcome anyone, so long as they are open to one simple idea: People with different beliefs really can set aside the labels and work to find common ground.

As we mentioned early in this book, 97 percent of Americans told us this year that it was important for our next president to be a problem solver. *97 percent.* 80 percent told us that we need one set of shared Democratic and Republican goals for our country when the next president takes office. Over the coming months and years, we're going to be on a campaign to answer that call.

We have to start now — we don't have any time to waste. Some have argued that redistricting or campaign finance reform can solve our troubles. And while these are admirable causes, we don't have the time to wait for them to gain momentum, pass into law, and finally kick into action. It could take decades — and we need a better government today. That means pushing our leaders to be better — to give us the kind of government our nation deserves. And if they won't, then the answer is to elect the leaders who will.

We can't simply accept a status quo where our government doesn't work. We should urgently insist that our best days can still be ahead of us — as long as our leaders actually start leading once again.

This won't be easy. But we're in this for the long haul. This is going to be a multiyear movement to ensure that the next American president is a problem solver and that he or she will have a problem-solving infrastructure in place to deal with once in office.

If we want this campaign to succeed in the days ahead, we're going to need partners like you. The next chance you have, please email **erin@nolabels.org** and tell us your top goals for our nation. Go to **NoLabels.org** and sign on to our campaign for a new, shared American vision. We'll keep in touch every step of the way because we want you to be involved throughout this process.

After the National Problem Solver Convention in New Hampshire, we'll be working to build a critical mass of 1 million Americans who endorse this idea. We'll also be working in Washington to get more and more members of Congress to sign onto the resolutions for a National Strategic Agenda in the House and Senate. Already, more than 70 members have. And we'll continue to press those seeking the 2016 presidency to embrace this new governing framework, one that actually provides specifics on *how* to be a problem-solving leader, not just talk like one.

As we've learned again and again, when the American people come together to call for something with one voice, the politicians start to listen. The more people who tell their leaders that we need a common purpose through shared goals, the sooner we can start to turn this ship around.

So please, join our campaign. Tell your leaders that enough is enough. And tell them that the next time you walk into the voting booth, you're not going to just rubber stamp the same politics of division and destruction. From now on, you're only going to vote for problem solvers. And if they want your vote, they had better stop fighting and start fixing.

CONNECT WITH NO LABELS

If you believe it's time for our leaders to start coming together around a national strategic agenda, then please get in touch and join our campaign. This is your movement – and we need your help to change politics for good.

SIGN UP TO JOIN THE MOVEMENT AT
NOLABELS.ORG

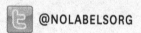 @NOLABELSORG

 FACEBOOK.COM/NOLABELS

NO LABELS:
A SHARED VISION FOR A STRONGER AMERICA

From America's most prominent political leaders and thinkers, a pathway to cut through the gridlock and make our government work.

Every year the President of the United States stands before Congress and the American people to deliver a State of the Union Address. What was once an opportunity for honest reflection on accomplishments and goals has become more of a laundry list than a speech—a grab bag of policy ideas, partisan rhetoric, and healthy dose of wishful thinking. Meanwhile, the gridlock in Washington means that virtually nothing in that speech will amount to anything but talk.

Governor Jon Huntsman and Senator Joe Manchin, two of the most respected and straightforward political leaders in America, have a simple solution for Washington's gridlock. It begins with getting our leaders together at the table to agree to goals not just for their party but for the whole country. Stop having one party led by the president paint a single vision. Instead, create a shared vision for our country to aspire to—and then find a way to achieve it together.

In *No Labels: A Shared Vision for a Stronger America*, Huntsman and Manchin are joined by experts and politicians from both sides of the aisle, including well-known thought leaders from business, economics, and academia. Contributors include two former White House Chiefs of Staff; former OMB Director Alice Rivlin; Glenn Hubbard, Dean of Columbia Business School; nine members of Congress committed to solving Washington's endemic problems, and many more contributors from every walk of life.

These contributors are all making a loud and strong call for a new process of running the United States of America. They believe in the cause of No Labels, and we believe you will, too.

JUST THE FACTS: THE FIRST STEP IN BUILDING A NATIONAL STRATEGIC AGENDA FOR AMERICA

Everyone knows our government is broken. But both our government and our country can be fixed if enough people come together to demand a new politics of problem solving.

That's what No Labels has believed since we first launched in 2010. Now, we have launched our most ambitious initiative yet. We're spending the next year organizing leaders inside and outside of Washington, as well as regular citizens, to tackle America's toughest challenges. This new National Strategic Agenda will be released in October 2015 and will set out a path for where America needs to go and how we get there.

Just the Facts will help guide the creation of the National Strategic Agenda by clarifying the essential facts, trends and assumptions that need to serve as the foundation for discussion of critical policy issues such as jobs, the budget, Social Security and Medicare and energy.

Politicians always tell us that we need to unite our nation. This book—and this new campaign for a National Strategic Agenda—can show us how.